40-Day Transformation Combo: Emotional Intelligence Guide & Success Mindset Manual

Dominic Blackwood

Table of contents

Introduction: The 40-Day Promise

Most people believe success depends on talent. They imagine that the people who move ahead faster simply have better ideas, stronger intelligence, or more natural ability. Talent certainly matters. Skill matters. Knowledge matters. But there is a quieter factor—less visible, rarely discussed with the same urgency—that determines whether talent actually turns into results. That factor is the ability to manage your internal world when pressure rises.

Imagine a professional who consistently performs at a high level. Their work is sharp, their thinking is fast, and their ambition is obvious to everyone around them. They are the person colleagues expect to succeed. They understand complex problems quickly. They generate strong ideas. On paper, they have everything needed to move forward.

But then something small happens.

A project deadline tightens unexpectedly. A colleague criticizes their proposal in a meeting. A client questions their judgment. The moment is uncomfortable, but not catastrophic. Still, something inside them reacts before logic has time to intervene. Frustration rises quickly. Their voice sharpens. They become defensive. The conversation turns tense. What could have been a simple exchange becomes an argument.

Later, the person replays the situation in their mind. They recognize what happened. They know they overreacted. They understand that the criticism was not a personal attack, but by that point the damage is already done. The opportunity to respond calmly has passed.

This kind of moment is far more common than people realize. It does not happen because someone lacks intelligence. It does not happen because they lack drive. It happens because raw ability, on its own, does not guarantee emotional control.

Many talented people unknowingly run their lives like a powerful engine without steering. They have energy, ambition, and capability, but when pressure appears, their reactions are automatic rather than intentional. Their emotions drive their decisions instead of informing them.

This gap rarely receives the attention it deserves.

Traditional success advice often focuses on productivity systems, discipline, networking strategies, or specialized knowledge. Those elements are valuable, but they assume something important already exists: the ability to regulate emotions, interpret setbacks accurately, and respond constructively in difficult moments.

Without those skills, even the most capable person can sabotage their own progress.

A talented employee may lose trust because they cannot manage frustration.
A brilliant entrepreneur may abandon promising ideas because early obstacles feel like personal failures.
A capable leader may damage team morale because they react impulsively under stress.

Over time, these patterns create a frustrating contradiction. From the outside, the person looks capable of far more than they achieve. From the inside, they feel as though something invisible keeps interfering with their progress.

That invisible factor is the relationship between emotional intelligence and mindset.

This book exists to address that relationship directly.

Over the next forty days, you will build two powerful capabilities at the same time. The first is emotional intelligence—the ability to understand your emotional reactions, regulate them effectively, and interpret the emotions of others with clarity. The second is mindset—the mental framework through which you interpret challenges, setbacks, and opportunities.

Many books teach one of these skills in isolation. This one does not.

Here, emotional intelligence and mindset are treated as two parts of the same system.

To understand why, it helps to look closely at how people actually experience daily life. Emotions are not separate from thinking; they shape it constantly. The interpretation you give to events influences your emotional reaction, and your emotional reaction influences the beliefs you form about yourself and the world.

Consider a simple example. A professional presents an idea that receives critical feedback. One person interprets the feedback as a signal that their thinking can improve. Their emotional response remains stable, and they refine their approach. Another person interprets the same feedback as proof that they are not respected. Their emotional reaction becomes defensive, and the opportunity to learn disappears.

The event is identical. The emotional outcome is completely different.

This difference does not come from intelligence. It comes from the interaction between emotional awareness and mental framing.

When these two elements work together, people respond to pressure with clarity rather than impulse. They recover from setbacks faster. They maintain stronger relationships. They remain focused on long-term goals even when short-term obstacles appear.

Research across leadership, psychology, and organizational performance consistently points to the same pattern. Individuals with high emotional intelligence tend to earn higher incomes, lead more effective teams, and report greater life satisfaction. However, those advantages appear most strongly when emotional intelligence is paired with intentional goal-setting habits and constructive mental frameworks.

In other words, emotional awareness without direction can become introspection without progress. At the same time, ambitious goal-setting without emotional awareness can lead to burnout, conflict, and poor decisions under stress.

The real leverage appears when both systems develop together.

That principle shapes the structure of this book.

Instead of separating emotional intelligence and mindset into different sections, the next forty days weave them together deliberately. Each concept you learn on one day reinforces the concept you encounter the next.

The rhythm is simple. Odd-numbered days focus on emotional intelligence skills. These days develop awareness, emotional regulation, empathy, and communication clarity. Even-numbered days focus on mindset shifts. These days reshape the way you interpret challenges, set goals, and frame your personal growth.

Each pair of days works as a small feedback loop.

You may begin by learning how to recognize a specific emotional trigger. The following day you will examine the belief system that gives that trigger its power. As the days progress, emotional awareness strengthens your mindset, and mindset adjustments stabilize your emotional responses.

Over time, the two systems begin reinforcing each other automatically.

The goal is not to eliminate emotions. Emotions are valuable signals. They highlight what matters, alert us to risk, and energize action. The goal is to ensure that emotions inform decisions rather than hijack them.

This transformation does not require years of intensive study. It requires consistent, focused practice applied in manageable steps.

That is why the journey is structured as a forty-day process.

Forty days is long enough to create meaningful psychological change but short enough to maintain commitment. The structure is divided into four phases, each lasting ten days and building directly on the previous one.

The first phase focuses on awareness. During these initial ten days, you will learn to observe your emotional patterns without judgment. Many people attempt to change their reactions before they fully understand them. Awareness corrects that mistake. By identifying emotional triggers, habitual thought patterns, and common stress responses, you create the foundation for meaningful change.

The second phase develops regulation. Awareness alone is not sufficient if emotional reactions still control behavior in critical moments. These ten days introduce practical tools for slowing impulsive responses, stabilizing emotional reactions, and maintaining composure under pressure.

The third phase introduces reframing. Once emotional stability improves, it becomes easier to examine the beliefs that shape your interpretation of events. In this phase, you will challenge limiting assumptions, strengthen resilience, and build a mindset that treats obstacles as information rather than threats.

The final phase focuses on integration. Skills learned separately must eventually function together in real situations. These final ten days help you apply emotional awareness and mindset shifts simultaneously so they become part of your natural decision-making process.

Each day follows the same simple format. You will spend approximately fifteen to twenty minutes reading a short concept explanation. Immediately afterward, you will complete a small practical exercise designed to apply the idea in your daily life.

These exercises are intentionally brief. Transformation does not come from occasional bursts of intense effort. It comes from small actions repeated consistently over time.

Think of each exercise as a mental repetition—similar to a single repetition in physical training. One repetition does not change the body immediately, but hundreds of repetitions gradually build strength. The same principle applies to emotional intelligence and mindset.

Consistency matters more than intensity.

Before beginning the first day, however, it is useful to establish a starting point. Most people have a vague sense of their emotional habits and mental patterns, but vague impressions make progress difficult to measure. A simple baseline assessment allows you to observe how much change occurs during the forty days.

Take a moment to reflect on three areas.

First, consider emotional awareness. When a strong emotion appears—anger, frustration, anxiety—how quickly do you recognize it? Do you notice the emotion as it arises, or only after it has already shaped your reaction?

Second, consider emotional regulation. When pressure increases or something goes wrong, how easy is it for you to regain composure? Do your reactions tend to escalate quickly, or can you pause before responding?

Third, examine your mindset toward challenges. When a setback occurs, what is your first interpretation? Do you see it primarily as evidence of limitation, or as feedback that helps you improve your approach?

Rate yourself honestly in each area on a simple scale from one to ten. The numbers themselves are less important than the reflection they encourage. These scores represent your starting point, not a judgment of your ability.

By Day 40, you will revisit these same questions. Most readers discover that their reactions to pressure, criticism, and uncertainty feel noticeably different. Situations that once triggered frustration or self-doubt begin to feel manageable.

That change does not happen because the world becomes easier. It happens because you learn to steer the powerful engine you already possess.

Talent opens doors. Emotional intelligence keeps them open. A strong mindset ensures you continue walking forward.

The next forty days are designed to help those three elements work together.

Chapter 1 — Know What You Actually Feel

1.1 — The Emotional Blind Spot

Most people believe they understand their emotions fairly well. After all, emotions feel obvious. When you are angry, you feel it in your body. When you are nervous, your thoughts speed up and your muscles tighten. When you are happy, energy rises and the world feels lighter. Because emotions appear so vivid and immediate, it is easy to assume that recognizing them is simple.

Yet in practice, many people move through their entire day with only a vague understanding of what they actually feel.

Ask someone how they are feeling during a difficult moment and the answers often sound similar: stressed, frustrated, annoyed, overwhelmed, tired. These words are not wrong, but they are extremely broad. They act like large containers that hold many different emotional experiences inside them. Because the labels are so general, they often hide more than they reveal.

Psychologists use a term for the ability to identify emotions with precision: emotional granularity. The phrase describes how specifically a person can distinguish one emotional state from another. Some people use only a handful of emotional labels to describe their internal experience, while others can recognize subtle differences between similar feelings.

Research suggests that most adults regularly use only five or six emotional categories in daily life. Words like stress, anger, happiness, sadness, and anxiety cover a wide range of internal states. But when researchers map the full landscape of human emotions, they identify dozens of distinct emotional experiences—more than thirty that appear consistently across studies.

This difference matters more than it might seem.

Imagine trying to navigate a large city using a map that shows only five roads. You might recognize the general direction you need to travel, but every decision becomes difficult. Intersections blur together. Landmarks are missing. Detours appear confusing because the map lacks detail.

The same thing happens internally when emotional language is limited.

If the only word you use for discomfort is stress, then anxiety, pressure, embarrassment, disappointment, and mental fatigue all collapse into a single category. When that happens, your brain loses valuable information. Instead of seeing what type of experience you are facing, you see only a vague signal that something is wrong.

And when the signal is vague, the response is often ineffective.

Consider a situation many people encounter at work. A manager gives unexpected feedback in front of colleagues. The comment is not harsh, but it is critical. Immediately, tension rises in the body. The heart rate increases slightly. Thoughts begin racing. The person leaves the meeting thinking, "I'm really stressed."

But what is the actual emotion?

Is it embarrassment from being corrected publicly? Is it anxiety about how others interpreted the moment?

Is it disappointment in personal performance? Is it insecurity about professional competence?

Each of these feelings is different, even though they may all feel uncomfortable. More importantly, each one requires a different response.

If the core emotion is embarrassment, the best response may involve reframing the moment and recognizing that public feedback is normal in collaborative environments. If the emotion is anxiety about reputation, the useful action might be to clarify expectations with the manager. If the emotion is disappointment, the response may involve improving a specific skill.

But if the experience is labeled simply as stress, none of these distinctions appear. The brain treats the entire situation as a generic threat. Instead of solving the underlying issue, the person may try to escape the discomfort entirely.

This is where many repeated mistakes begin.

People often react to emotions they have not correctly identified. When that happens, they attempt to solve the wrong problem. Because the real issue remains hidden, the same situation keeps appearing again and again.

One of the most common examples involves anger.

Anger is a powerful and visible emotion. It creates energy quickly and pushes people toward action. But anger is often not the first emotion in a chain of reactions. In many cases, anger appears after another emotion has already been triggered.

Someone might feel ignored in a conversation, which produces hurt. Hurt is uncomfortable and vulnerable, so the mind converts that feeling into anger. Anger feels stronger and more protective.

But once anger takes over, the original feeling disappears from awareness.

The result is a reaction that seems disproportionate to the situation.

A friend cancels plans at the last minute. Instead of acknowledging disappointment or feeling unimportant, the person becomes irritated and snaps at them. Later they may feel confused about why the reaction was so intense. From the outside, the anger appears unjustified. From the inside, it feels automatic.

This pattern happens constantly in everyday life.

People call exhaustion "stress." They call disappointment "anger." They call fear of uncertainty "lack of motivation." They call loneliness "irritation with others."

Each mislabeling shifts attention away from the real emotional signal. When the signal is misunderstood, the response becomes misaligned.

Over time, these small misunderstandings accumulate. Situations repeat. Reactions feel predictable. A person may begin to believe they simply have a "short temper" or a tendency to "overthink," when in reality the underlying issue is much simpler: their emotional vocabulary is too narrow to describe what is happening internally.

Emotional granularity changes this dynamic completely.

When people develop the habit of identifying emotions precisely, their brain begins to process experiences differently. Instead of reacting automatically, they pause long enough to interpret what is happening. That brief pause creates a space between the emotion and the reaction.

Inside that space, choice becomes possible.

The difference may seem subtle, but it is powerful. Neuroscience research shows that labeling an emotion accurately reduces the intensity of the emotional reaction itself. When the brain converts a raw feeling into language, it activates regions associated with cognitive control. The act of naming the emotion shifts part of the experience from the reactive system to the reflective system.

In practical terms, simply saying "I feel anxious about the uncertainty of this situation" can reduce the urgency of the anxiety compared to the vague statement "I'm stressed."

The mind moves from confusion toward clarity.

Clarity does not eliminate discomfort, but it transforms how the discomfort is interpreted. Instead of feeling like an overwhelming force, the emotion becomes information. It tells you something about your needs, expectations, or concerns.

The challenge is that most people have never practiced this skill deliberately.

Throughout childhood and adolescence, emotional education is rarely systematic. People learn words like happy, sad, and angry, but few environments encourage deeper emotional awareness. As a result, adults often reach high levels of professional competence while still using the emotional vocabulary they developed decades earlier.

They may have learned hundreds of technical terms related to their profession but only a handful that describe their internal world.

The good news is that emotional granularity can be developed quickly with practice.

The first step is learning to pause before labeling a feeling. Instead of accepting the first broad category that appears, you briefly examine the experience with curiosity.

What exactly is happening internally?

Is the sensation closer to anxiety or anticipation? Is the discomfort frustration, disappointment, or mental fatigue? Is the tension coming from pressure, uncertainty, or fear of evaluation?

These distinctions may seem small at first, but they change how the brain organizes the experience. The more specific the label becomes, the more precisely the brain can respond.

For example, consider the difference between saying “I’m overwhelmed” and saying “I’m mentally fatigued because I’ve been concentrating for several hours.” The first statement describes a vague emotional storm. The second identifies a specific cause that can be addressed directly, perhaps by resting or shifting tasks.

Accuracy transforms emotional signals into useful guidance.

Another important shift occurs when people stop treating emotions as problems that must immediately disappear. When emotions are labeled correctly, they often reveal understandable reasons for their presence. Feeling disappointed after missing an opportunity means you cared about the outcome. Feeling anxious before a new challenge means the situation matters to you.

Instead of interpreting these signals as weaknesses, you can treat them as indicators of what deserves attention.

Developing emotional granularity does not require memorizing dozens of emotion words overnight. It begins with a simple habit practiced repeatedly: pause and ask what you actually feel.

Not what you think you should feel. Not what sounds socially acceptable. Not the fastest label your mind can produce.

What is the most accurate description of your internal state right now?

At first, the answer may still be broad. That is normal. Precision grows gradually as attention improves. Over time, you begin to notice patterns. Certain situations produce predictable emotional combinations. Certain triggers repeatedly activate the same reactions.

When these patterns become visible, emotional reactions stop feeling mysterious.

This awareness is the foundation for everything that follows in this book. Every skill related to emotional intelligence—regulation, empathy, communication, resilience—depends on recognizing the emotional signal accurately in the first place.

If you cannot identify what you feel, you cannot choose how to respond to it.

But once you can name the experience clearly, the relationship between emotion and action begins to change. Instead of being carried by reactions you barely understand, you start steering them deliberately.

That shift begins with something surprisingly simple: learning to notice, pause, and say the right word for what is happening inside you.

1.2 — Body Signals as Data

Long before a person consciously recognizes an emotion, the body has already begun reacting to it. The heart rate shifts. Breathing changes. Muscles tighten or relax. The stomach contracts slightly. Even the temperature of the skin can fluctuate. These reactions happen automatically because emotions are not just mental experiences; they are full-body responses shaped by the nervous system.

Yet most people are trained to ignore these signals.

Modern life encourages attention to external demands—deadlines, conversations, notifications, responsibilities—while internal sensations fade into the background. A person may move through an entire day barely noticing how their body feels unless discomfort becomes extreme. By the time emotional reactions become obvious, they have often already reached a high intensity.

Learning to read body signals changes that pattern.

Your body acts like an early detection system for emotional shifts. It registers changes seconds or even minutes before the conscious mind interprets them. When you become skilled at noticing these signals, you gain access to valuable information earlier in the emotional cycle. Instead of discovering an emotion after it has already shaped your behavior, you notice it while it is still forming.

This awareness gives you time to respond deliberately rather than react automatically.

To develop this skill, it helps to understand that different emotional states tend to produce different physical signatures.

These signatures are not identical for every person, but certain patterns appear consistently.

Anxiety often shows up in the chest and breathing. People may feel a tightness in the upper chest or notice their breathing becoming shallow and rapid. The shoulders may lift slightly, and the body may lean forward as if preparing to respond to a threat.

Frustration often appears in the jaw, neck, or temples. The jaw tightens. Teeth may press together without the person realizing it. The forehead contracts slightly, and tension gathers around the eyes.

Embarrassment frequently produces warmth in the face or neck. The body may feel suddenly exposed or hyper-aware of other people's attention.

Sadness can bring heaviness to the chest or shoulders. Movements slow down. The body may feel heavier than usual, as if energy has drained away.

These physical reactions are not random. They are the nervous system preparing the body for action. Anxiety prepares the body to escape or solve a problem quickly. Anger prepares the body to confront a threat. Sadness slows the system down, encouraging reflection and withdrawal.

When people fail to notice these signals, emotional reactions can escalate quickly. The body moves from mild tension to strong agitation before the mind fully understands what is happening. But when these signals are observed early, the entire process becomes easier to manage.

One of the simplest ways to develop this awareness is through a brief body-scan practice.

The body scan is not complicated, and it does not require meditation experience. It simply involves directing attention through different parts of the body and observing sensations without trying to change them.

Take a moment to imagine doing this right now.

You begin by noticing your breathing. Not forcing it to slow down or deepen—just observing its natural rhythm. Is it shallow or deep? Fast or steady? Smooth or uneven?

Then your attention moves to your jaw. Are your teeth touching? Is there pressure between them? Many people discover they have been clenching their jaw without realizing it.

Next you notice your shoulders. Are they relaxed or lifted slightly toward your ears? Tension in the shoulders often signals accumulated stress that has not yet reached conscious awareness.

Then you shift attention to the chest and stomach. Is there tightness, heaviness, or a subtle knot in the stomach? Digestive tension is one of the most common early indicators of anxiety or anticipation.

Finally, you notice the hands and arms. Are they relaxed or slightly restless? Sometimes people find themselves gripping a pen, tapping their fingers, or tightening their fists when irritation is building.

This process takes less than a minute when practiced regularly, but it reveals an enormous amount of information.

What makes the body scan powerful is not just observation but interpretation. Over time, you begin connecting physical sensations with emotional states. The tight jaw becomes a signal that irritation may be forming. Shallow breathing becomes a sign of rising anxiety. A knot in the stomach may signal worry about an upcoming decision.

Gradually, your body becomes a map that tells you what is happening internally.

To strengthen this skill, it helps to create a simple personal emotion-body map. This exercise takes only a few minutes and provides a useful reference point for future awareness.

Think back to a recent moment when you felt frustrated. Instead of focusing on the situation itself, focus on your body. Where did you feel the frustration first? Was it in your chest, your jaw, your stomach, or somewhere else?

Write down the location of the sensation and how it felt physically.

Next recall a recent moment of anxiety or worry. Again, focus on the body rather than the story. Did your breathing change? Did your stomach tighten? Did your shoulders tense?

Record those sensations as well.

Finally, think of a moment when you felt calm or satisfied. Notice how the body felt in that state. Often breathing becomes deeper, muscles relax, and posture opens slightly.

By mapping these patterns, you begin recognizing the early signals of emotional change.

The goal is not perfect accuracy. Bodies are complex systems, and emotional signals can overlap. What matters is building the habit of noticing sensations before emotions intensify.

With practice, this awareness becomes surprisingly quick. A person may feel the first tightening of the jaw and immediately realize irritation is beginning to rise. Instead of waiting until anger appears in their voice, they can pause, breathe, and decide how to respond.

In this way, the body provides an early-warning system.

Most emotional reactions follow a predictable timeline. First comes a subtle physical signal. Then the emotion becomes recognizable. Finally the emotion influences behavior. If awareness enters the process early enough—during the physical signal stage—the entire reaction becomes easier to guide.

This is why emotional intelligence is not purely mental. It depends on listening to the body as much as the mind.

By learning to interpret these signals, you begin catching emotional reactions at their earliest stage. Instead of being surprised by your own reactions, you see them forming in real time.

That awareness creates the foundation for the next skill: understanding what situations trigger those reactions in the first place.

Chapter 2 — Rewrite the Stories You Tell Yourself

2.1 — The Narrative Loop

Every person walks through life with a quiet narrator in their mind. This narrator speaks constantly, interpreting events, explaining situations, predicting outcomes, and assigning meaning to almost everything that happens. Most of the time, this internal voice operates so smoothly that people barely notice it. It feels less like a voice and more like truth itself.

When something goes wrong, the narrator quickly explains why. When something goes well, it offers a reason for that too. The process feels automatic, almost invisible, yet it influences nearly every emotional reaction and decision a person makes.

Psychologists sometimes describe this pattern as a narrative loop.

The brain is built to interpret the world through stories. Raw information alone is not very useful to the human mind. Facts, events, and sensations become meaningful only when they are placed into a narrative that explains what they mean and what might happen next. These stories help the brain organize complexity and reduce uncertainty.

The problem is not that the brain tells stories. The problem is that the brain often tells protective stories rather than accurate ones.

The mind evolved to detect threats quickly. Long before modern workplaces or social networks existed, humans survived by anticipating danger and reacting rapidly to potential risks. The brain developed systems that favored caution and self-protection over objective analysis.

Those systems still operate today, even though the threats most people face are rarely life-threatening.

Instead of worrying about predators or physical danger, the modern brain reacts to social threats—criticism, rejection, embarrassment, uncertainty about status or belonging. When those situations appear, the mind immediately constructs a narrative designed to protect the person from potential harm.

These narratives often sound convincing because they appear instantly and feel emotionally charged. But many of them are distorted in subtle ways.

Someone might receive constructive criticism and immediately think, "I'm not good enough." Another person might see a colleague succeed and interpret it as proof that opportunities are disappearing. Someone else might notice a short email from a supervisor and assume they are about to be reprimanded.

None of these interpretations are guaranteed to be correct, yet the brain treats them as if they are facts.

This is how the narrative loop forms.

An event occurs. The mind quickly creates a story to explain it. The story produces an emotional reaction. That emotional reaction reinforces the story, making it feel even more believable.

Because the story feels true, it influences behavior. That behavior then shapes future experiences, often confirming the original narrative.

Over time, the loop strengthens itself.

For example, imagine a professional who quietly carries the belief that they are not as competent as others around them. The belief may have formed years earlier from a difficult experience—perhaps a failed project or criticism from an authority figure. The original moment may have passed long ago, but the story remained.

Whenever a challenging assignment appears, the narrative activates automatically.

The mind says something like, "You're going to struggle with this." The person approaches the task cautiously, maybe hesitating to ask questions or propose ideas. That hesitation limits their engagement. Because they participate less actively, their performance appears less confident. When the project ends without strong recognition, the brain interprets the result as confirmation.

The story repeats itself.

This process rarely happens consciously. Most people do not wake up and decide to believe limiting things about themselves. Instead, narratives quietly shape perception until they feel like simple observations.

To understand how powerful these internal stories can be, consider the experience of a mid-career professional named Daniel.

Daniel had spent more than fifteen years working in a technical field. He was reliable, knowledgeable, and respected by colleagues. Managers trusted him with complex projects, and he consistently delivered solid results. From the outside, his career looked stable and successful.

Yet something unusual had happened over the previous five years.

While many of his peers had moved into leadership roles or taken on larger strategic responsibilities, Daniel remained in the same position. His performance reviews were positive, but promotions seemed to pass him by. Occasionally a supervisor would encourage him to apply for a new opportunity, but he often hesitated.

When Daniel eventually worked with a leadership coach, the situation became clearer.

On the surface, Daniel believed that career advancement depended on timing and organizational politics. He assumed other people had simply been luckier. But during conversations about past experiences, a deeper narrative emerged.

Early in his career, Daniel had once presented an idea during a meeting with senior managers. The presentation did not go well. He struggled to explain the concept clearly, and one executive dismissed the proposal quickly. The moment embarrassed him deeply.

Although the situation was brief and quickly forgotten by others, Daniel's mind had formed a story about it. Without realizing it, he concluded that he was not someone who communicated ideas effectively in leadership settings.

That interpretation became part of his narrative identity.

Over the years, whenever opportunities appeared that involved presenting ideas, leading discussions, or influencing senior leaders, the narrative loop activated. Daniel's internal voice reminded him of the earlier experience. The message was subtle but persistent: "This isn't your strength."

Because of that belief, Daniel approached these situations cautiously. He spoke less frequently in meetings. He deferred to others when discussions became strategic. He focused on technical work where he felt safer.

None of this behavior was dramatic. It simply made him less visible when leadership opportunities appeared.

Managers evaluating potential candidates saw someone dependable but not necessarily influential. Promotions went to individuals who appeared more comfortable leading discussions and advocating for ideas.

Each time this happened, Daniel's narrative strengthened. His mind interpreted the lack of advancement as proof that he was correct about himself.

The loop continued for years.

What made the situation particularly striking was that Daniel's belief was not supported by evidence. When he finally examined his history objectively, he realized that the early presentation failure had been an isolated event during his first year in the company. In many other situations, he had communicated ideas effectively.

But the brain rarely compares stories with evidence once a narrative becomes familiar. Familiar stories feel safe because they create predictability, even when they limit growth.

Breaking the narrative loop requires recognizing that these internal stories exist in the first place.

Most people carry several recurring narratives about themselves and the world. Some are empowering, encouraging persistence and confidence. Others quietly restrict behavior.

Common limiting narratives appear in many forms.

Some people carry the belief that they are not naturally confident in social situations. Others believe they are always the person who must work harder than everyone else just to keep up. Some assume that authority figures are likely to judge them harshly. Others believe that success inevitably leads to criticism or pressure.

These stories rarely appear as dramatic statements. Instead they operate quietly in the background, shaping interpretation and reaction.

The first step in changing them is identifying them clearly.

To do that, it helps to observe situations that produce strong emotional reactions. When you notice frustration, anxiety, or self-doubt, pause and ask a simple question: what story is my mind telling about this moment?

Often the answer appears immediately.

Perhaps the story says that mistakes will damage your reputation. Perhaps it suggests that others are evaluating you more critically than they actually are. Perhaps it assumes that past outcomes predict future results.

When these stories are written down, patterns emerge quickly.

Most people discover that a small number of narratives repeat across many situations. Instead of dozens of different explanations, the mind usually relies on three or four familiar interpretations.

One story might revolve around competence: “I’m not as capable as people expect.”

Another might revolve around belonging: “People don’t really value my perspective.”

A third might revolve around risk: “If I try and fail, it will confirm my weaknesses.”

These narratives influence countless small decisions—whether to speak up, pursue an opportunity, ask for feedback, or try something unfamiliar.

By identifying them clearly, you gain the ability to question them.

This does not mean instantly replacing them with unrealistic optimism. The goal is not to pretend that challenges disappear. The goal is to examine whether the story you are telling yourself actually reflects reality.

In the coming chapters, you will learn methods for challenging and rewriting these internal narratives. But before that can happen, the stories themselves must become visible.

Take a moment now to reflect on situations where you consistently hesitate or feel uncertain. Notice the thoughts that appear automatically in those moments. Write down the explanations your mind offers.

When you review them together, you may notice that only a few core narratives appear again and again.

Those narratives are powerful not because they are true, but because they have been repeated often enough to feel true.

Recognizing them is the first step toward changing the loop.

2.2 — Cognitive Reframing in Practice

Once you begin noticing the internal narratives that shape your reactions, a natural question appears: what should you do when one of those narratives shows up?

Awareness alone is powerful, but it is only the first step. If the mind continues repeating the same interpretation every time a familiar situation appears, the narrative loop remains intact. The story might now be visible, but it still influences emotions and behavior.

Changing that loop requires a practical way to interrupt the automatic interpretation and replace it with something more accurate.

This is where cognitive reframing becomes useful.

Cognitive reframing is the process of examining a thought, testing its accuracy, and deliberately constructing a more balanced interpretation. The goal is not to force positive thinking or deny real challenges. Instead, the goal is to question whether the first explanation your brain provides is the most reasonable one.

Many automatic thoughts are shaped by fear, memory, or incomplete information. They are quick guesses, not verified conclusions. When they go unexamined, the brain treats them as facts.

A simple tool known as the Three-Column Method makes it easier to slow this process down.

The method works exactly as its name suggests. When you notice a strong emotional reaction, you briefly write three things.

First, you record the situation that triggered the reaction. This step keeps the exercise grounded in reality rather than drifting into abstract self-analysis. You describe what actually happened in clear, simple language.

Second, you write down the automatic thought that appeared in your mind. This thought often explains why the emotional reaction occurred. It may sound harsh, exaggerated, or pessimistic, but the goal is to capture it honestly rather than edit it.

Third, you examine the evidence and write a more balanced interpretation. This alternative thought is not forced optimism. It is a realistic explanation that considers the available evidence rather than assuming the worst.

The entire process can take less than two minutes once the habit becomes familiar.

What makes the method effective is that it moves the mind from reaction to analysis. Instead of allowing the narrative loop to run automatically, you briefly step outside it and examine the story.

To see how this works in everyday life, it helps to walk through several examples.

Imagine a professional named Sofia who works in marketing. She sends a proposal to her manager and receives a short response: “Let’s talk about this later.”

The situation is simple. Her manager wants to discuss the proposal.

However, Sofia immediately feels tension rising in her chest. Her mind produces an automatic thought: “The proposal must be bad. I probably missed something important.”

The emotion that follows is anxiety.

Using the Three-Column Method, Sofia writes the situation in the first column: manager asked to discuss proposal later.

In the second column she writes the automatic thought: the proposal is flawed and I made a mistake.

Now she pauses and considers the evidence before writing the third column. Her manager often schedules discussions when reviewing proposals. The message itself did not contain criticism. The proposal took careful preparation.

A more balanced interpretation appears: the manager may simply want to discuss details or provide feedback.

Notice that the alternative thought does not claim the proposal is perfect. It simply recognizes that the negative interpretation was not the only explanation.

The emotional intensity often decreases immediately when this shift occurs.

A second example might come from a personal relationship.

Consider someone named Marcus who notices that a close friend has not responded to his message for two days. The silence feels uncomfortable. His automatic thought becomes: "They must be upset with me."

That interpretation creates a sense of worry and tension.

Writing the situation clarifies the event: friend has not replied to a message.

The automatic thought appears in the second column: they are upset or avoiding me.

In the third column, Marcus examines other possibilities. His friend recently mentioned being busy at work. Messages sometimes get overlooked. There has been no conflict between them recently.

A balanced interpretation might be: the delay likely has nothing to do with me; they may simply be occupied.

Again, the goal is not to guarantee the best possible outcome. The goal is to widen the range of explanations so the mind stops assuming the worst one automatically.

A third example might involve health and personal habits.

Imagine someone trying to establish a new exercise routine. After missing two scheduled workouts in a busy week, a familiar thought appears: "I'm terrible at sticking with routines."

That statement feels factual because it draws on frustration from the moment.

But when written in the Three-Column Method, the situation becomes clearer: missed two workouts this week due to a crowded schedule.

The automatic thought is visible: I lack discipline and will probably quit again.

Now the person examines evidence. In the previous month they exercised consistently most weeks. The missed workouts happened during an unusually busy period.

A balanced interpretation might read: this week was difficult, but past weeks show I can maintain the habit when my schedule stabilizes.

The emotional reaction changes from discouragement to problem-solving.

The same process works in financial situations as well.

Imagine someone reviewing their monthly expenses and realizing they spent more than expected. A wave of concern appears, followed by a familiar narrative: "I'm terrible with money."

When written down, the situation becomes specific: spent more this month due to several unexpected expenses.

The automatic thought becomes visible: I have no financial discipline.

But evidence may reveal something different. Most months the budget is balanced. This month included a medical bill and a necessary repair.

A balanced interpretation might say: this month exceeded the budget because of unusual costs; adjusting next month's spending will restore balance.

In each of these examples, the initial thought felt convincing because it appeared quickly and carried emotional weight. The Three-Column Method interrupts that speed. Writing the thought slows the process enough for the analytical part of the mind to participate.

Once the brain examines evidence rather than reacting automatically, the narrative loop begins to loosen.

Another important benefit of this method is that it externalizes thinking. When thoughts remain inside the mind, they often blend together with emotions. Writing them down separates the interpretation from the experience.

A thought that felt like a solid truth can suddenly look exaggerated or incomplete when it appears on paper.

Over time, repeated practice builds a new habit. The mind becomes quicker at noticing distortions even without writing them down. Eventually the internal conversation begins to sound different.

Instead of immediately believing the first interpretation, a second question appears almost automatically: what evidence supports this story?

That simple question is enough to weaken many limiting narratives before they fully take hold.

This skill does not eliminate emotional reactions. Emotions still arise, especially in situations that matter deeply. But the reaction becomes shorter and more manageable because the story behind it receives scrutiny.

The more frequently you practice this process, the more flexible your thinking becomes. Instead of being trapped inside familiar narratives, you begin adjusting them based on new information.

That flexibility leads directly into the next idea: the understanding that beliefs themselves are not permanent truths.

Chapter 3 — Master the Pause Before Reaction

3.1 — The Six-Second Rule

Everyone has experienced a moment they wish they could take back.

A sentence spoken too sharply in the middle of an argument. An email sent quickly in frustration. A reaction during a meeting that felt justified in the moment but embarrassing afterward. These moments often share the same pattern. Something happens quickly, an emotion surges just as quickly, and the response appears before the rational mind has time to evaluate the situation.

Later, when the emotional intensity fades, the reaction seems unnecessary or exaggerated. The person may even struggle to understand why they reacted that way at all.

This pattern is not a character flaw. It is a biological process.

To understand it, we need to look at what happens in the brain during strong emotional reactions. The human brain is not a single unified system making calm, balanced decisions. It is a network of different regions that evolved at different times, each responsible for different functions.

One of the most important structures involved in emotional responses is the amygdala. The amygdala is a small, almond-shaped cluster of neurons located deep within the brain. Its primary job is to detect potential threats and prepare the body to respond quickly.

For most of human history, this system helped people survive real physical dangers. When early humans encountered a predator or another immediate threat, there was no time for careful analysis. The body needed to react instantly. The amygdala triggered a cascade of physiological responses that prepared the body for action: increased heart rate, sharpened attention, and the release of stress hormones.

This rapid reaction system still exists today.

The problem is that the brain does not distinguish perfectly between physical danger and emotional discomfort. Social threats—criticism, embarrassment, perceived disrespect, uncertainty about status—can activate the same alarm system.

When the amygdala detects a threat, it sends signals that trigger the release of chemicals such as adrenaline and cortisol. These chemicals prepare the body to react quickly. The process happens in fractions of a second, often before the thinking part of the brain has evaluated the situation.

Psychologist Daniel Goleman famously described this phenomenon as an "amygdala hijack."

During an amygdala hijack, the emotional brain temporarily overrides the rational brain. Instead of thoughtful decision-making, the body shifts into a reactive state. Attention narrows, the heart beats faster, breathing becomes shallow, and the mind prepares for confrontation or defense.

In modern life, this reaction rarely helps.

Instead of escaping a predator, the person may respond to a colleague, partner, or family member in a way that damages the relationship. Instead of improving the situation, the reaction intensifies it.

What makes this process especially interesting is the timing.

The chemical surge triggered by the amygdala does not last forever. The initial wave of stress hormones moves through the bloodstream quickly, and it begins to dissipate within a short window of time. Researchers studying emotional reactions have found that the most intense phase of this response lasts only a few seconds.

In many cases, the surge peaks within roughly six seconds.

Those six seconds represent a critical window. During that brief period, the emotional brain is pushing the body toward reaction. If the reaction happens immediately, the emotion controls the outcome. But if the person can pause long enough for the chemical surge to settle, the rational brain regains influence.

This is where the idea of the six-second rule becomes useful.

The rule is simple: when a strong emotional reaction begins, create a pause of at least six seconds before responding.

That small pause allows the brain to move out of pure reaction mode. The prefrontal cortex—the part of the brain responsible for reasoning, planning, and impulse control—has time to re-engage.

In practical terms, six seconds can mean the difference between an impulsive reaction and a thoughtful response.

Consider a moment when someone criticizes your work during a meeting. The comment feels unfair, and your immediate impulse may be to defend yourself quickly. If you respond instantly, the emotional reaction may dominate the conversation. Your tone might sharpen, and the discussion could become confrontational.

But if you pause for six seconds, something subtle happens. The intensity of the emotional surge begins to decline. The thinking part of your brain becomes active again. Instead of reacting defensively, you may choose a calmer response, such as asking a clarifying question or acknowledging the feedback before explaining your perspective.

The difference is not dramatic in terms of time, but it can be enormous in terms of outcome.

Of course, pausing in the middle of an emotional moment is easier said than done. When the body is flooded with adrenaline, the urge to react feels urgent. That is why it helps to have simple techniques that make the pause easier to create.

One of the most effective techniques involves controlled breathing.

Breathing is unique because it is both automatic and voluntary. Normally the body breathes without conscious effort, but you can also influence the rhythm intentionally. When breathing slows down, it sends signals to the nervous system that reduce the intensity of the stress response.

A technique known as box breathing is especially useful during emotional moments.

The idea is simple. You inhale slowly for four seconds, hold the breath for four seconds, exhale for four seconds, and then hold again for four seconds before repeating the cycle. The rhythm resembles the four equal sides of a box, which is where the name comes from.

This breathing pattern forces the body to slow down. The deliberate pace interrupts the automatic stress response and helps regulate the nervous system. Even one cycle of box breathing lasts sixteen seconds, which is more than enough time for the initial chemical surge to begin fading.

Another technique involves using a physical anchor.

A physical anchor is a small physical action that grounds your attention in the present moment. The action can be almost invisible to others, but it provides a sensory reference point that helps interrupt the emotional reaction.

For example, you might press your thumb and forefinger together gently and focus on the sensation of contact. You might place both feet firmly on the ground and notice the pressure of the floor beneath them. Some people rest a hand lightly against a table or chair and pay attention to the texture of the surface.

These small physical sensations anchor the mind in the present moment. Instead of being carried away by the emotional surge, attention shifts to something stable and neutral.

The anchor creates just enough distance between the emotion and the reaction.

A third technique is even simpler: silent counting.

Counting slowly in your mind creates a structured pause. When emotions rise quickly, the mind tends to move rapidly through thoughts and interpretations. Counting interrupts that momentum by introducing a steady rhythm.

Silently counting from one to six may sound almost trivial, but it creates the exact window needed for the amygdala surge to settle.

Some people prefer counting slightly longer, perhaps to ten, but the important point is that the counting is slow and deliberate. Each number becomes a moment of stillness before action.

These techniques work because they create time.

In emotional situations, time is the missing ingredient. Reactions happen quickly because the body moves faster than conscious thought. By inserting a small pause, you allow the rational brain to catch up with the emotional brain.

Over time, practicing this pause becomes a micro-habit.

A micro-habit is a behavior so small that it becomes almost automatic. Instead of trying to control every emotional reaction directly, you focus on one simple rule: pause before responding.

The pause does not need to be dramatic. It may look like a single breath, a moment of silence, or a short shift in posture. Most people around you will not even notice it.

But internally, that moment can transform the entire situation.

When the pause becomes habitual, emotional reactions begin to feel less overwhelming. Instead of being swept into the surge automatically, you begin recognizing the moment when the reaction starts.

You notice the tightening in your chest or jaw. You remember the six-second rule. You breathe, count, or anchor your attention briefly.

Then you respond.

This shift may seem small, but it represents one of the most important skills in emotional intelligence. The ability to pause before reacting protects relationships, improves decision-making, and prevents many unnecessary conflicts.

In the chapters ahead, you will build additional tools for managing emotions and shaping your mindset. But all of those tools depend on one basic ability: creating space between the trigger and the reaction.

And sometimes, that space is only six seconds wide.

3.2 — Responding vs. Reacting

The pause you learned in the previous section is not an end in itself. Its purpose is to create a moment of choice.

Without that moment, behavior tends to follow a predictable pattern. A trigger appears, an emotion rises, and the body moves directly into action. Words come out quickly. Decisions happen in the heat of the moment. The reaction may feel justified, even necessary, but it often reflects the emotional surge rather than the situation itself.

This is what it means to react.

Reacting is automatic. It is the body's fast protective response to perceived threats. The mind attempts to defend status, avoid embarrassment, or push back against pressure. Because the reaction is quick, it rarely includes careful evaluation. It is driven by urgency.

Responding is different.

Responding still includes emotion, but it also includes awareness. Instead of letting the emotional surge determine the outcome, the person acknowledges the emotion and then chooses an action deliberately. The difference between reacting and responding is not the absence of feeling. It is the presence of intention.

You can think of reacting as reflexive and responding as strategic.

Reflexes are useful in situations that require immediate physical action. If a glass falls from a table, your hand moves automatically to catch it. The brain does not analyze the situation first. It simply acts.

But in social and professional environments, reflexive reactions often create unnecessary problems. Conversations become tense. Small misunderstandings escalate into arguments. Feedback feels like a personal attack instead of useful information.

Responding introduces a different rhythm.

When you respond, you allow the situation to unfold for a moment before choosing how to engage with it. That short delay allows the thinking brain to evaluate the context, the relationship, and the potential consequences of different actions.

A useful way to remember this shift is through a simple decision pathway: Trigger, Pause, Label, Choose, Act.

Every emotional situation begins with a trigger. A trigger can be almost anything—a comment from a colleague, a message from a supervisor, a mistake in a project, or a disagreement at home. The trigger itself is neutral. It is simply the event that starts the chain of reactions.

Immediately after the trigger, the pause appears. This is the six-second window you practiced earlier. The pause interrupts the automatic reaction long enough for awareness to enter the situation.

Once the pause exists, the next step is labeling the emotion. Instead of letting the feeling operate invisibly, you identify it clearly. Perhaps you notice irritation rising in your chest, or anxiety tightening your breathing. Naming the emotion brings it into conscious awareness.

After labeling the emotion, you reach the most important step: choosing.

Choosing means asking a quiet but powerful question. What outcome do I want from this situation? Not what emotion is pushing me toward, but what result would actually improve the situation.

Sometimes the answer might involve asking a question instead of making a statement. Sometimes it might involve listening more carefully before responding. In other cases, it may mean setting a boundary or expressing disagreement calmly.

Finally, after that brief process, you act.

The action may look similar to what a reaction would have produced, but the tone and intention will be different. Because the choice was deliberate, the response tends to align with long-term goals rather than momentary emotion.

To see how this decision pathway works in practice, imagine a common workplace situation.

A manager reviews your work during a meeting and points out a problem in front of others. The trigger appears immediately: public criticism.

Without awareness, the reaction might be defensive. You might interrupt the manager quickly to explain why the criticism is unfair. The tone becomes tense, and the conversation shifts away from solving the problem.

But if you follow the decision pathway, something different happens.

The trigger still appears, but you pause. You take one slow breath. The emotional surge begins to settle.

You then label the feeling internally: irritation mixed with embarrassment. Naming the emotion prevents it from operating unconsciously.

Next you ask what outcome you actually want. In most cases, the goal is not to win the moment but to maintain credibility and move the project forward.

With that perspective, you choose a response. Perhaps you say, "That's helpful feedback. Let me explain the reasoning behind that section so we can adjust it if necessary."

The conversation remains constructive, and the situation stays professional.

The difference between reacting and responding is rarely dramatic from the outside. It is often only a matter of tone and timing. But those small differences shape how others experience the interaction.

People who react frequently appear volatile or defensive. People who respond thoughtfully appear composed and reliable, even in difficult situations.

This distinction becomes especially important during high-stakes moments.

Consider a difficult conversation with a partner or family member. Emotions may already be heightened. If one person reacts quickly, the other often reacts in return, and the discussion escalates rapidly.

But if one person pauses and responds instead, the emotional temperature of the conversation changes. The pause disrupts the escalation cycle.

The same pattern appears during feedback sessions at work. When someone receives criticism, the instinct to react defensively can block useful learning. A pause followed by a thoughtful response allows the conversation to remain productive.

Crises provide another example.

During unexpected problems—a missed deadline, a financial setback, a mistake in a project—people look to leaders for signals about how to respond. Leaders who react impulsively create confusion and tension. Leaders who pause and respond deliberately create stability.

The decision pathway becomes even more valuable in these moments because it provides a clear mental structure.

Trigger, Pause, Label, Choose, Act.

At first, this sequence may feel slow or unnatural. The mind is accustomed to reacting immediately. But with practice, the process becomes surprisingly quick. The steps happen internally within seconds.

Eventually, the pathway becomes automatic in the same way reactions once were.

Instead of moving directly from trigger to reaction, your mind begins inserting the pause and evaluation almost without effort. Emotional intelligence starts operating in real time.

That transformation requires practice, which leads to the next step: integrating the pause habit into everyday life.

Chapter 4 — Set Goals That Survive Bad Days

4.1 — Why Most Goal Systems Fail

At the beginning of a new year, a new project, or a new phase of life, many people make the same promise to themselves. This time will be different. This time the habits will stick. The plan will be followed. The energy will last longer than the first wave of enthusiasm.

For a while, it often works.

The new routine begins with energy. A person wakes up earlier to exercise, tracks expenses more carefully, or dedicates time to learning a new skill. The first days feel productive and hopeful. The effort seems manageable because motivation is high and the goal feels meaningful.

But then something ordinary happens.

A stressful week at work appears. Sleep becomes irregular. A small setback interrupts the routine. Maybe a meeting runs late, a dcadlinc shifts uncxpcctcdly, or pcrsonal rcsponsibilitics increase for a few days. The new habit becomes slightly harder to maintain.

One missed day turns into two.

Soon the original plan begins to fade. The person might tell themselves they will restart next week or next month, but the momentum has disappeared. What felt like a promising change slowly returns to the background of daily life.

This pattern is so common that it has become almost predictable.

Research on New Year's resolutions illustrates the problem clearly. Studies consistently show that a large percentage of people abandon their resolutions within the first few weeks of the year. Some surveys suggest that nearly a quarter of resolutions disappear by the end of January, and a majority fail before the year reaches its halfway point.

These statistics are often interpreted as evidence that people lack discipline. The story usually goes something like this: if individuals simply had more willpower, they would follow through on their plans.

But the reality is more complex.

Most goal systems fail not because people lack effort, but because the systems themselves are fragile. They are designed for ideal conditions rather than real life. They assume that motivation will remain stable, that emotions will stay manageable, and that daily routines will remain predictable.

In reality, none of those conditions are guaranteed.

Life is full of interruptions, stress, fatigue, uncertainty, and emotional turbulence. A goal that survives only when conditions are perfect will collapse quickly when conditions become messy.

To understand why so many goals fail, it helps to examine three common weaknesses that appear in many popular goal-setting methods.

The first weakness is vagueness.

A vague goal sounds inspiring but offers little guidance for action. Someone might say they want to “get healthier,” “save more money,” or “improve their career.” These statements express direction, but they lack clarity about what actually needs to happen each day.

When goals remain vague, progress becomes difficult to measure. Without clear indicators, the mind struggles to determine whether effort is sufficient or whether adjustments are needed.

Vagueness also makes it easier for the brain to delay action. If the goal is simply to “exercise more,” almost any level of activity can appear acceptable in the moment. The mind finds ways to interpret the goal flexibly, which often leads to postponing effort until tomorrow.

This problem led to the popularity of structured frameworks such as SMART goals, which encourage goals to be specific, measurable, achievable, relevant, and time-bound. These frameworks improved clarity, but clarity alone does not guarantee consistency.

This leads to the second weakness: motivation-dependent execution.

Many goal systems assume that people will act consistently because they want the outcome strongly enough. The assumption is that motivation will drive behavior day after day. When enthusiasm fades, the person simply needs to remind themselves why the goal matters.

In practice, motivation is unpredictable.

Emotional states fluctuate constantly. Some mornings begin with energy and optimism, while others begin with fatigue or anxiety.

Some days feel productive and focused, while others feel scattered and heavy.

A goal system that depends on motivation works only when motivation appears. On difficult days, when emotions are unstable or energy is low, the system loses its power.

This is why many habits feel effortless during the first week of a new plan but become increasingly difficult as daily stress accumulates. The original enthusiasm fades, and the goal suddenly requires effort without emotional support.

When the brain senses this discomfort, it often chooses the easiest path in the moment.

This dynamic reveals the third weakness: the absence of an emotional contingency plan.

Most goal systems focus on what actions should happen, but they rarely address what happens when emotions interfere with those actions. Yet emotions are one of the most powerful forces shaping behavior.

Frustration, fatigue, self-doubt, boredom, and stress all influence how people approach their goals. When these emotions appear, they can weaken motivation quickly.

Consider a simple example involving a new exercise routine.

During the first week, enthusiasm makes the routine enjoyable. The person feels motivated and proud of the effort. But after several days of poor sleep and heavy workload, the body feels tired. The emotional state shifts from excitement to resistance.

If the goal system depends entirely on motivation, this moment becomes a turning point. The person skips one workout, telling themselves they need rest. The next day feels equally demanding, and another workout disappears.

The routine collapses not because the goal was unrealistic but because the system did not anticipate emotional fluctuations.

Human behavior is deeply influenced by feelings in the moment. A system that ignores this reality will eventually fail.

That is why sustainable goals must be emotion-proof.

Emotion-proof goals are not immune to feelings, but they are designed to survive them. Instead of assuming that motivation will remain constant, they acknowledge that some days will be difficult.

An emotion-proof system asks a different question.

Instead of asking, “What should I do when everything feels easy?” it asks, “What will I do when I feel tired, discouraged, or distracted?”

When goals include answers to that question, they become far more resilient.

For example, instead of relying on willpower alone, a person might design routines that reduce the need for decision-making. Preparing exercise clothes the night before removes friction in the morning. Scheduling a short walk rather than an intense workout creates a backup plan for low-energy days.

These adjustments may appear small, but they address the emotional reality of human behavior.

Another important shift occurs when people stop treating missed days as evidence of failure. Traditional goal systems often assume a perfect streak of success. When a disruption occurs, the person interprets it as a sign that the plan is not working.

Emotion-proof systems expect disruptions.

Instead of requiring perfect consistency, they focus on rapid recovery. The system answers a simple question: what is the smallest action that keeps the goal alive when motivation disappears?

If the goal involves writing, the smallest action might be a few sentences instead of several pages. If the goal involves exercise, the smallest action might be a ten-minute walk instead of a full workout.

These actions maintain momentum even when conditions are not ideal.

Momentum matters because the brain interprets continuity as progress. When the chain of effort remains intact, even in reduced form, it becomes easier to return to full effort later.

The difference between fragile goals and resilient goals is not ambition. Both may aim for meaningful change. The difference lies in how the system handles emotional turbulence.

Fragile goals assume the path will be smooth. Resilient goals prepare for rough terrain.

Understanding this distinction changes how you think about achievement.

Success rarely comes from perfect conditions or uninterrupted motivation. It emerges from systems that continue functioning even when emotions fluctuate. People who maintain long-term progress are not necessarily more disciplined than others. Often they simply use goal systems that remain stable during difficult days.

They expect interruptions. They anticipate fatigue. They design routines that survive stress.

In the next sections of this chapter, you will learn how to build goals that operate this way. Instead of relying on enthusiasm alone, you will create structures that continue moving forward when motivation fades.

Because in the long run, the goals that succeed are not the ones that look impressive on paper.

They are the ones that survive bad days.

4.2 — The EQ-Aligned Goal Framework

Once you understand why many traditional goal systems collapse, the next step is building a structure that can survive real life. Most goal-setting advice focuses heavily on clarity and measurement, but it rarely addresses the emotional dimension of progress. Yet emotions play a decisive role in whether a goal continues or disappears.

A plan that looks perfect on paper can still fail if it does not account for discouragement, frustration, fatigue, or uncertainty. Goals exist inside human lives, not inside spreadsheets. They must function in the presence of unpredictable moods, interruptions, and stress.

This is why effective goals need to be aligned with emotional intelligence.

An emotionally intelligent goal system does not simply define what you want to achieve. It also anticipates how you will feel during the process and prepares responses for those moments. Instead of assuming motivation will remain steady, it builds emotional resilience directly into the structure of the goal.

One of the clearest ways to organize this kind of system is through a simple hierarchy: values, vision, milestones, and daily actions.

At the foundation of this structure are values. Values represent the deeper principles that guide how you want to live and what you consider meaningful. They are not temporary motivations or external rewards. Instead, they describe the direction you want your life to move in over time.

Examples of values might include personal growth, creativity, financial stability, health, family connection, or contribution to others. These ideas may sound abstract, but they serve an important purpose. When goals connect directly to values, they feel more stable. The goal is no longer just about achieving a result; it becomes an expression of something that matters to you.

Without this connection, goals often drift toward external benchmarks. People pursue achievements because they seem impressive or socially expected rather than personally meaningful. When the emotional cost of effort increases, those externally motivated goals lose their power quickly.

Values provide a deeper reason to continue.

Once values are clear, the next level of the hierarchy is vision. Vision describes how those values might appear in your life if you developed them consistently over time. It translates abstract principles into a picture of what the future could look like.

For example, someone who values personal growth might imagine becoming a confident communicator who can explain ideas clearly in professional settings. Someone who values health might imagine living with energy and physical strength that supports daily activities. Someone who values financial stability might picture a life with reduced financial stress and greater freedom to make long-term decisions.

Vision is not about perfection. It is simply a direction that helps guide daily choices.

The next layer of the framework is milestones. Milestones break the vision into meaningful progress points that can be reached within a realistic timeframe. In this book, the focus is a forty-day cycle. A milestone might therefore represent something that can reasonably improve within those forty days.

For instance, a milestone connected to the value of personal growth might involve speaking up at least once during professional meetings. A milestone related to health might involve establishing a consistent exercise rhythm several times per week. A milestone related to financial stability might involve tracking spending habits and identifying areas for improvement.

Milestones provide a sense of movement. They show that progress is happening even when the larger vision remains distant.

Finally, daily actions translate milestones into specific behaviors that can occur each day or week. Daily actions are the smallest building blocks of change. They may appear modest, but their cumulative effect creates the milestone over time.

The key difference in the EQ-aligned framework is that each milestone also includes an emotional contingency plan.

Traditional goal-setting systems often focus exclusively on actions: what to do, when to do it, and how to measure it. But they rarely ask an equally important question: what will you feel when the process becomes difficult?

Every meaningful goal eventually produces emotional resistance. At some point motivation fades, doubts appear, or progress feels slower than expected. When that moment arrives, people often interpret the discomfort as evidence that the goal is unrealistic or that they lack the necessary discipline.

In reality, emotional turbulence is a normal part of progress.

An emotionally intelligent goal system anticipates this moment instead of being surprised by it. For each milestone, you ask two additional questions.

First, what emotion am I most likely to experience when this goal becomes difficult? The answer might be frustration, boredom, self-doubt, or fatigue.

Second, what is my planned response to that emotion?

For example, imagine someone working toward the milestone of writing regularly. The most likely emotional obstacle might be discouragement when ideas do not flow easily. The contingency plan might involve a simple rule: write for ten minutes even when the writing feels imperfect.

Another example might involve financial goals. A person may anticipate feeling anxious or overwhelmed when reviewing expenses. The emotional plan might include a routine of reviewing numbers calmly once per week rather than avoiding them.

These emotional contingency plans transform the goal from a fragile intention into a resilient process. Instead of interpreting emotional resistance as a signal to stop, the person already knows how to respond.

At this stage of the book, the goal is not to design dozens of objectives but to focus on three meaningful goals that can be pursued during the forty-day period. Each goal should connect to a value that genuinely matters to you. Each should include a milestone that can realistically move forward during the next six weeks. Each should also identify the emotional challenge that will likely appear.

By writing these elements together, the structure becomes clear.

The value provides meaning.
The vision provides direction.
The milestone provides measurable progress.
The daily action provides momentum.
The emotional plan protects the goal when motivation weakens.

This framework ensures that goals are not merely intellectual decisions. They become integrated with emotional awareness and realistic planning.

Over time, this alignment creates a powerful effect. Instead of abandoning goals when emotions fluctuate, you expect those fluctuations and continue anyway. Progress becomes steadier because the system supports you during difficult moments rather than collapsing under them.

Chapter 5 — Read Rooms and Build Trust

5.1 — Social Awareness as a Superpower

Some people walk into a room and immediately understand what is happening beneath the surface.

They can sense tension even when no one has raised their voice. They notice when a colleague's enthusiasm is genuine and when it is forced. They detect subtle shifts in attention during meetings and adjust their communication accordingly. These individuals seem to read situations almost instinctively.

To others, these interactions may appear confusing or unpredictable. A conversation suddenly becomes awkward and they cannot explain why. A proposal receives polite agreement, yet later fails to gain support. A team meeting ends with apparent consensus, but hidden resistance emerges afterward.

The difference between these experiences often comes down to one skill: social awareness.

Social awareness is the ability to perceive emotional and relational signals within a group. It involves recognizing what people are feeling, how they are reacting, and how power and influence are moving through the room—even when none of those dynamics are spoken directly.

Many people assume this skill belongs only to naturally charismatic personalities. In reality, social awareness is largely a matter of attention.

Most of the signals that reveal group dynamics are visible to everyone in the room. They appear in facial expressions, tone of voice, body language, and conversational patterns. The problem is not that the signals are hidden. The problem is that people often become so focused on their own thoughts that they stop noticing the environment around them.

When someone enters a meeting while mentally rehearsing what they plan to say, they may overlook valuable information. While they concentrate on presenting their idea, they miss the moment when two colleagues exchange a skeptical glance. While they prepare their next point, they fail to notice that another participant's posture has shifted from interest to disengagement.

These small signals form a quiet language of interaction.

People rarely state their feelings directly in professional or social settings. Instead, their reactions appear through subtle changes in expression, timing, and tone. Learning to notice these changes provides a remarkable advantage because it allows you to respond to the real situation rather than the one you assume exists.

Consider a common workplace scenario.

A team gathers to discuss a new initiative. One person presents an idea enthusiastically, and several colleagues nod politely. From the presenter's perspective, the meeting appears successful. People seem supportive, and no one openly disagrees.

Yet beneath the surface, something different is happening.

One colleague briefly tightens their lips when the timeline is mentioned. Another glances toward a senior manager before speaking, as if checking whether their opinion is safe to express.

Two participants exchange a quick look when a specific budget figure appears.

These moments may pass quickly, but they carry meaning. They signal hesitation, concern, or disagreement that has not yet been spoken aloud.

Someone with strong social awareness notices these signals.

They might pause and ask a question about the timeline, inviting people to express concerns earlier. They might acknowledge the budget issue and encourage discussion before resistance grows quietly. By responding to subtle cues, they address problems while the conversation is still flexible.

Without that awareness, the discussion continues as if everything is aligned. The real objections appear later, often in private conversations or delayed decisions.

Social awareness therefore functions as an information advantage.

While others rely only on explicit statements, socially aware individuals receive additional signals about the emotional and relational landscape. They see where agreement exists, where uncertainty is forming, and where tension may develop.

This advantage does not require extraordinary intuition. It simply requires observing three categories of signals consistently: faces, voices, and interaction patterns.

The first step is scanning faces.

Human faces communicate emotion rapidly, often before words appear. Small movements around the eyes, mouth, and forehead reveal reactions that people may not intend to show. These expressions can change within fractions of a second, which is why they are sometimes called micro-expressions.

You do not need to analyze every expression in detail. The goal is simply to notice shifts.

For example, when someone introduces a new idea in a meeting, glance briefly around the room. Do people lean forward with interest, or do their expressions tighten slightly? Does anyone look surprised or concerned? Are there individuals who remain neutral while others show enthusiasm?

These observations help you understand the emotional climate of the discussion.

The second step involves listening for tone shifts.

Words alone rarely reveal the full meaning of what someone is saying. Tone of voice often carries more information than the sentence itself. A statement such as "That's interesting" can express curiosity, skepticism, or polite dismissal depending on how it is delivered.

Tone shifts can signal changes in emotion or confidence.

Someone who begins speaking slowly and clearly but then speeds up may be becoming nervous or defensive. A voice that drops slightly in volume may indicate uncertainty or hesitation. A sudden increase in energy may signal enthusiasm or urgency.

When you listen carefully to tone, conversations become richer in meaning.

Instead of interpreting statements only by their literal content, you begin hearing the emotional context behind them. This awareness allows you to respond more accurately.

The third step is noticing interaction patterns—specifically, who speaks to whom.

In any group, communication rarely flows randomly. People tend to direct their attention toward individuals whose opinions carry weight. Subtle patterns reveal alliances, influence, and social hierarchies.

For example, during discussions you might notice that several participants look toward a particular person after presenting an idea. That glance suggests the person holds informal authority. Even if they are not leading the meeting, their reaction influences how others interpret the conversation.

You might also notice that certain individuals consistently support each other's points or build on each other's comments. This pattern often indicates an alliance or shared perspective within the group.

Observing these dynamics helps you understand how decisions may unfold.

If you present an idea without recognizing who holds influence, you may miss the opportunity to engage the people whose support matters most. When you understand the relational structure of the room, you can communicate more strategically.

The three steps—scanning faces, listening for tone shifts, and observing interaction patterns—work best when practiced together.

Imagine attending a meeting where a proposal is being evaluated. As the presenter describes the plan, you briefly scan the faces around the table. Two participants appear attentive, but another frowns slightly when the timeline is mentioned.

You listen carefully to the next response. A colleague says, “That could work,” but their tone carries hesitation rather than enthusiasm.

Then you notice that several people glance toward the department director before commenting further.

These signals reveal a subtle dynamic. Some participants may have concerns about the timeline, and the group is waiting to see how the director responds before expressing stronger opinions.

With this awareness, you might ask a question that opens the discussion: “It seems like the timeline might raise some concerns. Would it help to review the phases more closely?”

The question acknowledges what people are already sensing but have not yet articulated.

Moments like this build trust because they show that you are attentive to the group rather than focused only on your own contribution. People feel understood when their unspoken concerns are recognized.

Social awareness therefore serves two purposes at once.

First, it provides information that helps you navigate complex interpersonal situations. Second, it communicates respect and attentiveness, which strengthens relationships over time.

Developing this skill requires patience. At first, you may notice only a few signals during conversations. With practice, your perception will sharpen. You will begin recognizing patterns that once passed unnoticed.

You may notice when enthusiasm in a room begins fading, or when someone wants to speak but hesitates. You may detect early signs of disagreement before it becomes open conflict.

These observations do not require you to manipulate or control situations. Instead, they allow you to engage with greater awareness.

In the chapters ahead, you will learn how to use this awareness to build deeper trust and influence within groups. But the first step is learning to see the room clearly.

When you begin paying attention to faces, tone, and interaction patterns, conversations stop feeling mysterious.

The signals were always there. Now you know how to notice them.

5.2 — Empathy Without Burnout

Social awareness allows you to notice what is happening in a room. Empathy allows you to respond to those signals in a way that strengthens connection rather than simply observing it.

When people speak about empathy, they often treat it as a single emotional skill. In reality, empathy has several forms, and understanding the difference between them is essential if you want to maintain emotional balance while still connecting with others.

Many people assume empathy means feeling exactly what another person feels. If someone else is anxious, you absorb their anxiety. If they are frustrated, you begin feeling frustrated as well. This experience is often described as emotional empathy.

Emotional empathy can create powerful moments of connection. When someone is grieving, distressed, or struggling, sensing their emotions deeply can make them feel seen and understood. However, emotional empathy also has a hidden cost.

When you absorb other people's emotional states repeatedly, your own emotional system becomes overloaded. Over time, this can lead to fatigue, irritability, and a sense of emotional exhaustion. Professionals in caregiving roles—teachers, therapists, healthcare workers, and managers—often experience this problem when they try to carry the emotional weight of everyone around them.

The challenge becomes even greater in leadership roles. When multiple people look to you for guidance, absorbing each person's emotional state can quickly become overwhelming.

This is why it helps to distinguish emotional empathy from another form known as cognitive empathy.

Cognitive empathy is the ability to understand what another person is experiencing without necessarily absorbing their emotional state. Instead of feeling the emotion directly, you recognize it, interpret its meaning, and respond appropriately.

Imagine a colleague explaining that they feel anxious about an upcoming presentation. Emotional empathy might cause you to feel anxious alongside them. Cognitive empathy, by contrast, allows you to understand their concern while remaining calm.

You might say something like, "It sounds like the presentation feels high-stakes for you. That makes sense. Would it help to walk through the structure together?"

In this moment, you are fully attentive to their experience. You understand the emotion and acknowledge it. But you do not become overwhelmed by it.

Cognitive empathy is sustainable because it maintains a boundary between understanding and absorption.

That boundary does not make the connection weaker. In fact, it often makes the support more effective. When you remain emotionally steady, you are better able to offer clarity, reassurance, or practical help.

This distinction becomes especially important in environments where emotional intensity is common. In workplaces facing pressure, families navigating conflict, or communities dealing with uncertainty, people naturally share their frustrations and concerns with those they trust.

If empathy means absorbing every emotion around you, the emotional burden becomes too heavy. If empathy means understanding those emotions while remaining grounded, you can support others consistently without losing your own balance.

One practical technique for maintaining this balance is known as the empathy bracket.

The empathy bracket involves creating a clear beginning and ending for moments of emotional engagement. When someone shares a concern, you intentionally step into their perspective for a defined period. You listen carefully, ask thoughtful questions, and acknowledge their feelings.

During this period, your attention is fully focused on understanding them.

However, when the conversation ends, you consciously return to your own emotional baseline rather than continuing to carry their feelings with you.

Think of it like opening and closing a bracket in a sentence. The bracket contains the emotional engagement. Once it closes, you return to the broader context of your own emotional state.

This practice can feel unusual at first because many people believe empathy requires continuous emotional involvement. In reality, the ability to step in and out of emotional engagement is what makes empathy sustainable.

Consider a situation where a team member approaches you with frustration about a project. You listen carefully while they describe the problem. You acknowledge the difficulty and ask clarifying questions.

During this interaction, you are fully present.

But once the conversation concludes, you pause briefly and take a breath before returning to your next task. That small reset signals to your mind that the emotional engagement has ended.

Without that reset, the mind may continue replaying the conversation and carrying the frustration forward.

The empathy bracket is particularly useful in environments where multiple emotional conversations happen throughout the day. Managers, teachers, and caregivers often move from one discussion to another quickly. Without a clear boundary, the emotional residue from earlier interactions can accumulate.

A short reset between conversations prevents this buildup.

The reset does not require anything elaborate. Sometimes a few slow breaths are enough. Other times it might involve standing up, stretching, or briefly shifting attention to a neutral task.

The important point is that the transition is intentional.

Over time, this technique creates a healthier rhythm. You become capable of deep listening and understanding without feeling drained afterward.

People around you still experience your empathy. They feel heard and respected. But your own emotional energy remains stable.

This balance allows you to maintain supportive relationships without sacrificing your well-being.

Empathy then becomes not just an emotional reaction but a skillful form of attention—one that strengthens connection while preserving personal resilience.

5.3 — Trust as Compound Interest

Trust is often described as something fragile. It can take years to build and moments to break. While this description captures part of the truth, it can also make trust feel mysterious or unpredictable.

In reality, trust usually develops through a much simpler process.

Think of trust as a form of compound interest.

When you deposit money into a savings account consistently, the balance grows gradually. Each deposit may appear small, but over time the accumulation becomes significant.

Trust works in a similar way. Each interaction with another person creates a small deposit or withdrawal. When deposits happen consistently—through reliability, honesty, and respect—the relationship grows stronger.

These deposits rarely come from dramatic gestures. They come from small, repeated actions.

Returning a message when you say you will return it is a deposit. Following through on a commitment is a deposit. Acknowledging someone's effort or perspective is a deposit.

Individually these actions may seem minor, but together they create a sense of predictability and safety. People begin to trust that your words align with your actions.

Over time this consistency becomes part of your reputation.

When someone who has built trust enters a conversation, others assume positive intentions. Even disagreements are interpreted with more generosity because the relationship already contains a strong balance of credibility.

But just as deposits build trust, certain behaviors quickly create withdrawals.

One of the fastest ways to damage trust is inconsistency. When a person behaves reliably one day and unpredictably the next, others become uncertain about what to expect. This uncertainty weakens confidence in the relationship.

Another common trust-destroyer is gossip. Speaking negatively about others when they are not present signals that the same behavior could occur again in different circumstances. Even if the gossip appears harmless, it creates a subtle sense of caution.

Over-promising also damages trust quickly. When someone makes commitments they cannot realistically fulfill, the gap between expectation and outcome grows larger with each interaction. Eventually people begin discounting their promises entirely.

Defensiveness creates a similar effect. When mistakes occur—and they inevitably do—defensiveness prevents honest discussion. Instead of addressing the issue directly, the conversation becomes a struggle over blame. This pattern discourages openness and slows learning.

A final trust-destroyer is the lack of acknowledgment. When people contribute ideas, effort, or time without recognition, they begin to feel invisible. Even small acknowledgments signal that their presence matters.

Avoiding these behaviors is not complicated, but it requires awareness.

Trust grows through patterns rather than isolated moments. A single positive interaction may create goodwill, but lasting trust comes from repeated experiences of reliability and respect.

This is why trust-building often appears quiet rather than dramatic.

A colleague who consistently arrives prepared for meetings builds trust gradually. A friend who keeps promises reliably builds trust through everyday actions. A leader who listens carefully and communicates transparently builds trust through steady presence.

These small deposits accumulate.

The compounding effect becomes visible during challenging moments. When a relationship contains a strong foundation of trust, people are more willing to give each other the benefit of the doubt. They assume misunderstandings can be resolved rather than assuming negative intentions.

This resilience makes collaboration easier.

Imagine two teams facing a difficult deadline. One team has developed trust through consistent reliability and open communication. The other team operates with uncertainty and skepticism.

When pressure increases, the first team works through problems more smoothly because members trust each other's intentions. The second team may struggle with tension and second-guessing because that trust has not been established.

The difference does not come from talent alone. It comes from the accumulation of small relational deposits.

Trust also grows through transparency. When people communicate openly about challenges or limitations, others understand the situation more clearly. Transparency prevents misunderstandings that might otherwise erode confidence.

For example, if a project timeline becomes difficult to maintain, acknowledging the challenge early allows the group to adjust expectations. Waiting until the last moment often creates frustration and confusion.

Transparency signals respect.

Another important trust-building habit involves acknowledging the contributions of others. Recognition does not need to be elaborate. Sometimes a simple statement of appreciation communicates that someone's effort is noticed.

These small acknowledgments reinforce the sense that the relationship matters.

Over time, people who consistently practice these behaviors develop a quiet reputation for reliability. Others begin seeking their input, inviting them into discussions, and trusting their judgment.

Trust becomes a form of social capital.

Like financial capital, it grows gradually through consistent investment. Each reliable action adds to the balance. Each respectful conversation strengthens the relationship.

When you approach trust in this way, it becomes less mysterious. You do not need dramatic gestures or charismatic speeches to earn confidence. You simply need to treat each interaction as an opportunity to make a small deposit.

Those deposits accumulate.

And over time, the relationships around you become stronger because of them.

Chapter 6 — Turn Failure Into Fuel

6.1 — The Failure Narrative Trap

Failure rarely damages people as much as the story they tell about it.

When a setback happens, the event itself is usually brief. A presentation goes poorly. A project is rejected. A job opportunity disappears. A financial decision does not work out. These moments may be uncomfortable, but they pass quickly in objective time.

What often lingers much longer is the interpretation that follows.

The human mind is wired to search for meaning. Whenever something unexpected or painful occurs, the brain begins asking questions almost immediately. Why did this happen? What does it say about me? Will it happen again?

These questions are natural, but the answers the brain produces are not always accurate. In many cases, the mind constructs a narrative that extends the meaning of the event far beyond what the evidence supports.

Instead of interpreting the situation as a temporary outcome, the brain begins linking it to identity.

A single failure becomes evidence of a personal limitation.

This process is what psychologists sometimes refer to as the failure narrative trap.

The trap begins with a simple cognitive shift. The mind stops describing what happened and starts describing who you are. The language changes from events to identity.

Instead of thinking, "This project failed," the thought becomes, "I'm not capable of managing projects like this." Instead of "That presentation did not go well," the narrative becomes, "I'm terrible at presenting."

These conclusions feel convincing because they emerge from emotional experiences. When embarrassment, frustration, or disappointment is present, the mind searches for explanations that seem to match the intensity of those feelings.

Unfortunately, the explanations often exaggerate the scope of the event.

The brain tends to generalize quickly. One negative outcome is interpreted as evidence of a broader pattern. A setback that occurred under specific conditions becomes a statement about overall ability.

Once this narrative forms, it begins influencing future behavior.

Imagine someone who experiences a difficult meeting in which their idea receives criticism. The emotional reaction may include embarrassment or self-doubt. If the mind constructs the narrative that they are not good at presenting ideas, the next opportunity to speak in a meeting becomes more stressful.

Anticipation of failure increases anxiety. Anxiety affects performance. Performance may then suffer again, reinforcing the original belief.

In this way, the narrative becomes self-reinforcing.

The original setback may have been temporary or situational, but the identity story creates a pattern that extends far beyond the initial moment.

To understand how powerful this process can be, consider two different individuals who experience nearly identical setbacks.

The first story involves a professional named Laura.

Laura worked in a mid-level management position within a growing company. She had built a reputation as a reliable contributor and had recently been given the opportunity to lead an important internal initiative. The project involved coordinating multiple departments and presenting progress updates to senior leadership.

For several weeks, Laura invested significant effort into the project. She prepared detailed reports, organized meetings, and tried to keep everyone aligned. However, the initiative encountered unexpected complications. Two departments disagreed about priorities, and the timeline began slipping.

During a progress presentation to senior leaders, the discussion became tense. Questions arrived rapidly, and Laura struggled to explain the delays clearly. One executive criticized the project plan openly, suggesting that the coordination had been weaker than expected.

The meeting ended quickly, and the project was reassigned to another team.

For Laura, the experience felt deeply discouraging. She replayed the meeting repeatedly in her mind. Each time she remembered the criticism, the same thought appeared: “I’m not capable of leading initiatives at this level.”

That thought gradually became a narrative.

Over the following months, Laura avoided opportunities that involved visible leadership. When new projects appeared, she focused on smaller operational tasks where expectations felt safer. Her confidence decreased, and colleagues began seeing her as someone who preferred supportive roles rather than strategic ones.

The initial event lasted less than an hour. The narrative that followed shaped her career for years.

Now consider another professional named Daniel who experienced a similar situation.

Daniel was also given the responsibility to lead a complex project. Like Laura, he encountered coordination challenges between departments. During a progress meeting with leadership, his explanation of the delays did not go smoothly. Several questions exposed weaknesses in the plan.

The meeting was uncomfortable.

Daniel left feeling frustrated and disappointed. But his interpretation of the situation developed differently.

Instead of concluding that the experience revealed a permanent weakness, he began asking different questions. What specifically made the presentation difficult? Were the questions about communication, preparation, or project structure?

Over the following days, he reviewed the situation with a mentor who had more experience managing cross-department initiatives. Together they identified several practical lessons. The timeline had been overly optimistic. Communication between teams needed clearer checkpoints. The presentation could have included more transparent updates about risks.

The event became a source of information rather than a verdict about Daniel's ability.

The next time Daniel led a project, he applied these lessons. The second experience was not perfect, but it improved. Over time, the earlier setback became part of his learning process rather than a defining moment.

The contrast between these two stories illustrates the difference between event interpretation and identity interpretation.

Both individuals experienced a setback. Both faced criticism and disappointment. The difference emerged in how the experience was framed internally.

Laura's narrative connected the event to her identity. The story became, "This happened because I am not capable." Daniel's narrative separated the event from identity. The story became, "This happened because certain parts of the process did not work."

The first narrative closes the door to improvement. The second keeps the door open.

What makes the failure narrative trap so powerful is that it operates quietly. Most people do not consciously decide to interpret setbacks in damaging ways. The brain simply produces explanations that feel emotionally consistent with the moment.

Embarrassment becomes evidence of incompetence. Frustration becomes evidence of inability. Disappointment becomes evidence that success is unlikely.

Over time, these interpretations accumulate into a self-concept.

When someone begins believing they are naturally bad at certain activities, they approach those situations with caution or avoidance. That reduced engagement limits opportunities for improvement, which reinforces the original belief.

Breaking the failure narrative trap begins with one important distinction.

Every setback contains two separate elements: the event and the meaning assigned to it.

The event consists of observable facts. A proposal was rejected. A conversation went poorly. A goal was not achieved within the expected timeframe.

The meaning involves interpretation. It answers the question of what the event says about your ability, potential, or identity.

When these two elements blend together, failure narratives emerge. The event and the interpretation become inseparable.

Separating them requires deliberate awareness.

When something goes wrong, begin by describing the event in neutral language. What actually happened? Which factors contributed to the outcome? What conditions influenced the situation?

This step prevents the mind from jumping immediately to identity-based explanations.

Next, examine the interpretation that appears automatically. Notice the story forming in your mind. Does it describe a permanent trait or a temporary situation? Does it assume the outcome represents your overall ability?

Often you will discover that the narrative contains assumptions rather than evidence.

Once those assumptions become visible, they can be questioned. Instead of asking, “What does this say about me?” you can ask, “What information does this event provide?”

This shift transforms failure from a verdict into feedback.

Feedback may still be uncomfortable, but it is useful. It identifies gaps in preparation, communication, strategy, or timing. Those gaps can be addressed through learning and adjustment.

When failure becomes feedback, it loses its power to define identity.

The event remains real, but its meaning changes.

Over time, practicing this separation builds resilience. Setbacks still occur, but they no longer carry the same emotional weight. Instead of triggering identity-based doubt, they become part of the ongoing process of improvement.

The difference may seem subtle, but it shapes how people approach challenges throughout their lives.

Some individuals allow setbacks to define who they believe they are. Others treat the same setbacks as information about what to refine next.

The event may be identical.

The story determines the outcome.

6.2 — The After-Action Review for Life

When a setback occurs, most people react in one of two ways. Some avoid thinking about the experience entirely. They move forward quickly, hoping the uncomfortable memory fades with time. Others replay the moment repeatedly in their minds, analyzing every detail with a mixture of frustration and self-criticism.

Neither response produces much learning.

Avoidance prevents reflection, which means valuable information disappears along with the memory. Rumination keeps the experience emotionally alive without producing clear conclusions. The mind circles around the same thoughts again and again without moving toward improvement.

There is a better alternative, and it comes from an environment where learning from mistakes is not optional.

In the military, teams regularly conduct something called an after-action review. After completing a mission or training exercise, participants gather to examine what happened. The goal is not to assign blame or protect reputations. The purpose is to extract lessons while the experience is still fresh.

The process works because it replaces emotional interpretation with structured reflection.

Instead of asking vague questions such as "Why did this go wrong?" the review follows a clear sequence. Participants identify the original objective, examine what actually occurred, discuss what they experienced during the event, and determine how future actions should change.

This structure can be adapted easily to personal development.

Think of it as a four-part reflection process that transforms any setback into a learning event. The questions are simple, but answering them honestly produces surprising clarity.

The first question is straightforward: what was the goal?

Before examining what went wrong, it is important to remember what you were trying to accomplish. This step anchors the reflection in the original intention. Sometimes the mind exaggerates failure because it forgets the realistic scope of the goal.

Perhaps the objective was to deliver a clear presentation, resolve a disagreement constructively, complete a challenging task, or maintain a new habit under pressure. Writing the goal down helps separate intention from outcome.

The second question follows naturally: what actually happened?

This is the factual portion of the review. The key is to describe events without inserting interpretation. Instead of writing statements like "I handled it poorly," focus on observable details.

You might write that the presentation ran longer than planned, that the conversation became tense after a particular comment, or that preparation was shorter than expected due to competing responsibilities. The purpose is to reconstruct the sequence of events as accurately as possible.

This step prevents the mind from collapsing the entire situation into a vague judgment.

The third question introduces emotional awareness: what did I feel during the experience?

Emotions often shape decisions in the moment, but they are rarely examined afterward. Identifying them explicitly reveals how they influenced behavior.

You might recall feeling anxious before speaking, defensive when challenged, or discouraged when progress slowed. These emotions are not signs of weakness; they are data about the internal environment in which decisions occurred.

Recognizing them makes it easier to prepare for similar situations in the future.

The final question completes the process: what will I do differently next time?

This is where learning becomes practical. The goal is not to produce a long list of criticisms but to identify a small number of adjustments that could improve the outcome.

Perhaps the next presentation will include clearer visual structure. Perhaps a difficult conversation will begin with a clarifying question rather than an immediate defense. Perhaps preparation time will be scheduled earlier to avoid last-minute pressure.

The change does not need to be dramatic. Often a small adjustment produces a meaningful difference.

To see how this method works in practice, imagine someone named Elena who recently experienced a difficult meeting with her team.

Elena had been responsible for presenting a new workflow proposal intended to streamline a process within her department. She believed the proposal was well thought out, but the meeting quickly became tense. Several colleagues expressed concerns, and the conversation ended without agreement.

Instead of replaying the moment emotionally, Elena decides to conduct an after-action review.

She begins by writing the goal. Her intention had been to explain the proposal clearly and receive feedback that would allow the team to refine it.

Next she describes what happened. The presentation lasted longer than expected, which left less time for discussion. One colleague raised concerns about implementation complexity, and the conversation shifted toward defending the idea rather than exploring it.

Then she identifies the emotions she felt during the meeting. She remembers feeling confident at the beginning but gradually becoming defensive as criticism appeared. That defensiveness caused her to respond quickly rather than listening carefully.

Finally, she writes what she will do differently next time. She decides that future presentations will include a shorter explanation followed by earlier invitations for feedback. She also notes that pausing to ask clarifying questions may prevent defensive reactions.

Within a few minutes, the experience has transformed from an emotional memory into a learning resource.

The meeting did not become successful retroactively, but its value increased because it produced insight. Instead of becoming a lingering frustration, the event became part of Elena's skill development.

This is the real purpose of the after-action review.

It protects experiences from being wasted.

Every setback contains information about preparation, communication, decision-making, or emotional responses. Without structured reflection, that information often disappears. With a simple review process, the same event becomes a source of improvement.

The method also weakens the failure narrative trap discussed earlier in the chapter. By focusing on specific elements of the situation, the mind stops interpreting the event as a statement about identity.

The experience becomes a case study rather than a personal verdict.

Over time, repeating this process builds a habit of constructive reflection. Instead of avoiding difficult moments or obsessing over them emotionally, you examine them with curiosity.

The question changes from “Why did this happen to me?” to “What can this experience teach me?”

That shift turns failure into fuel.

Chapter 7 — Communicate With Impact

7.1 — Difficult Conversations Made Simple

Most people do not struggle with communication during easy moments. When conversations are friendly, when everyone agrees, and when the stakes feel low, words flow naturally. The real challenge appears when something uncomfortable must be said.

A colleague's work is not meeting expectations. A friend repeatedly crosses a boundary. A manager asks for something unrealistic. In these situations people often experience a familiar tension between honesty and harmony. They want to express the truth, but they also want to avoid conflict or damaging the relationship.

As a result, many difficult conversations never happen.

Instead of addressing the issue directly, people soften the message until the meaning disappears. They hint rather than speak clearly. They delay the discussion until frustration builds. Sometimes they avoid the conversation entirely.

When that happens, the problem rarely disappears. It simply moves underground. Misunderstandings grow quietly, resentment accumulates, and small issues eventually become larger ones.

The challenge is not that people lack courage. It is that they lack a reliable structure for these conversations. Without a framework, emotions can easily take control. Words come out too sharply, or they become so cautious that the point never arrives.

A helpful way to approach difficult conversations is through a structure known as the STATE framework. The letters represent a sequence that helps keep communication both honest and respectful: share facts, tell your story, ask for their story, talk tentatively, and encourage dialogue.

Each step prevents one of the common mistakes people make during tense conversations.

The first step is sharing facts. When people begin difficult discussions with conclusions or accusations, the other person often becomes defensive immediately. Statements such as "You never listen" or "You don't care about this project" interpret behavior rather than describing it.

Facts, by contrast, describe observable events.

For example, instead of saying "You're always late to meetings," someone might say, "In the last three team meetings you arrived after the discussion had already started." This phrasing focuses on specific moments rather than character judgments.

Facts create a neutral starting point. They reduce the chance that the other person will feel attacked before the conversation has even begun.

After establishing facts, the next step is telling your story. This is where interpretation appears, but it is framed carefully. You explain what those facts mean from your perspective without presenting the interpretation as the only possible truth.

For example, after describing the late arrivals, you might say, "When that happens, I worry that we may not be fully aligned before decisions are made."

Notice the difference in tone. The statement describes an interpretation, but it also leaves room for other explanations.

The third step involves asking for their story. Difficult conversations become productive when both perspectives are visible. Asking for the other person's view signals that you are interested in understanding rather than simply delivering criticism.

A simple question such as "How do you see the situation?" invites them to share information you may not have considered.

Often this step reveals important context. Perhaps the colleague has been dealing with overlapping responsibilities or unclear scheduling. Perhaps the friend did not realize how their behavior affected you.

Understanding their perspective does not mean abandoning your own concerns. It simply creates a fuller picture of the situation.

The fourth element is talking tentatively. This does not mean weakening your message but expressing it with intellectual humility. Instead of presenting your interpretation as absolute, you present it as a thoughtful observation open to discussion.

Language such as "It seems like…" or "I may be mistaken, but…" keeps the conversation flexible. The other person feels less pressure to defend themselves because the message is not framed as a final verdict.

Finally, the conversation should encourage dialogue. Difficult discussions often stall because one person speaks while the other prepares a defense. Encouraging dialogue means inviting collaboration in solving the problem.

Questions such as “What do you think would help here?” or “How can we improve this moving forward?” shift the conversation from blame toward progress.

The STATE framework helps structure conversations that might otherwise feel overwhelming. But frameworks become useful only when people know how to apply them in real situations.

Consider the first scenario many people dread: giving critical feedback.

Imagine you are responsible for reviewing a colleague’s work. Their recent project contains errors that will affect the team’s progress if they continue.

Without a framework, the conversation might begin with frustration. You might say something like, “This report isn’t good enough,” which invites immediate defensiveness.

Using the STATE approach, the discussion sounds different.

You begin by sharing facts. You might say, “I noticed that several data points in the report did not match the figures from last week’s update.”

Then you tell your story. “When that happens, I become concerned that our final presentation could include inaccuracies.”

Next you ask for their perspective. “Can you walk me through how the numbers were gathered?”

The colleague may explain that the source data changed shortly before the deadline. Now both of you understand the situation more clearly.

Talking tentatively allows room for collaboration. "It seems like we may need an extra verification step before the next report."

Encouraging dialogue completes the exchange. "What process would help you check the numbers more efficiently?"

The feedback remains honest, but the conversation stays constructive.

Another conversation people often avoid involves setting a personal boundary.

Boundaries become necessary when repeated behavior begins affecting your well-being. For example, imagine a friend who frequently cancels plans at the last minute.

Without structure, frustration may eventually appear in a burst of criticism: "You never respect my time."

The STATE framework allows the message to remain calm and clear.

You begin with facts. "Over the past few weeks our plans have been canceled shortly before we were supposed to meet."

Then you share your story. "When that happens, I feel discouraged because I value the time we spend together."

Next you ask for their perspective. "Is there something about the scheduling that has been difficult lately?"

Talking tentatively keeps the conversation balanced. "I may be misunderstanding, but it seems like the timing might not be working well."

Finally, encourage dialogue. “How can we plan in a way that works better for both of us?”

The boundary becomes clear without turning the conversation into a confrontation.

A third scenario often produces the most anxiety: saying no to someone in authority.

Many people fear that declining a request from a supervisor or senior colleague will appear disrespectful or uncooperative. As a result, they accept commitments they cannot realistically fulfill.

The STATE framework provides a respectful way to communicate limits.

Imagine a manager asks you to take on an additional project while you are already managing several priorities.

You begin by sharing facts. “Right now I’m working on the quarterly report, the client presentation, and the system update scheduled for next week.”

Then you tell your story. “Taking on another project immediately could affect the quality of those commitments.”

Next you ask for their perspective. “How urgent is the new project compared with the current priorities?”

Talking tentatively maintains respect. “It seems like we may need to adjust something if I’m going to give the new task the attention it deserves.”

Finally, encourage dialogue. “Would you prefer that I shift focus from one of the existing projects, or should we schedule the new work for later in the week?”

The response communicates responsibility rather than resistance.

These examples illustrate how structure changes the emotional tone of communication. Difficult conversations remain difficult, but they become manageable when guided by clear principles.

Practicing these patterns gradually builds confidence. The language begins to feel natural rather than rehearsed. Over time, people discover that honest conversations often strengthen relationships instead of damaging them.

Clarity reduces misunderstanding. Respectful dialogue creates mutual understanding. Problems that once lingered unspoken can be addressed before they grow larger.

In the next sections of the chapter, you will expand these communication skills further. But the essential idea remains simple.

Difficult conversations do not require perfect words.

They require a clear structure that keeps honesty and respect moving in the same direction.

7.2 — Listening That Changes Relationships

Most people believe they are good listeners. In reality, what many people practice is not listening but waiting.

While another person is speaking, the mind often begins preparing a response. Thoughts appear quickly. You compare their experience with your own, search for advice you could offer, or silently evaluate whether you agree with what they are saying. By the time the speaker finishes, you already know what you plan to say next.

This habit feels natural because conversations usually move quickly. Yet it produces a form of listening that remains on the surface.

Surface-level listening focuses primarily on the words being spoken. The listener hears the information and may respond appropriately, but deeper elements of the message often go unnoticed. Emotional signals, underlying concerns, and subtle meanings can disappear beneath the literal content of the conversation.

People sense this difference immediately, even if they cannot explain it.

When someone listens only to respond, the interaction feels transactional. The conversation moves forward, but the speaker may not feel truly understood. When someone listens more deeply, the atmosphere changes. The speaker feels heard, and the conversation becomes more meaningful.

This deeper approach is sometimes described as Level-3 Listening.

Level-1 listening focuses mainly on the listener's internal thoughts. While another person speaks, the listener is mostly aware of their own reactions and ideas. This is the kind of listening that happens when you are distracted or impatient.

Level-2 listening focuses on the words and information being shared. The listener pays attention to the content and may ask relevant questions, but attention remains primarily on the facts of the conversation.

Level-3 listening goes further.

Instead of focusing only on words, the listener pays attention to emotion, tone, and the meaning behind the message. They notice how the speaker feels about what they are describing. They listen not just to understand the story but to understand the person telling it.

When someone practices Level-3 listening, they become aware of subtle signals that often pass unnoticed. The speaker's voice may slow down when discussing something difficult. A sentence may contain hesitation that suggests uncertainty. A change in posture or energy may reveal excitement or concern.

These signals provide context that words alone cannot fully express.

Consider a simple example. A colleague says, "The project has been challenging lately."

A Level-2 listener might respond by asking for more details about the tasks involved. A Level-3 listener notices the tone behind the statement. Perhaps the colleague sounds tired or discouraged. Instead of focusing only on the logistics, the response may address the emotion: "It sounds like it has been exhausting. What part has been the most difficult?"

This small shift invites a deeper conversation.

The power of Level-3 listening lies in its ability to make people feel understood without requiring complex advice or solutions. Often the speaker does not need immediate answers. They simply need to know that their experience has been recognized.

Practicing this kind of listening requires slowing down your internal dialogue. Instead of thinking about what you will say next, you allow the speaker's message to unfold fully before responding.

One effective way to develop this skill is through a simple partner exercise.

Imagine sitting with a friend, colleague, or partner. One person speaks for three minutes about something currently on their mind. It could be a challenge at work, a recent success, or a situation that feels confusing.

During those three minutes, the listener does not interrupt or ask questions. Their only task is to pay attention to the speaker's emotional signals.

When the three minutes end, the listener responds—but with one important restriction. They may not summarize the story or the content. Instead, they reflect only the emotions they heard.

The listener might say something like, "I heard excitement when you described the opportunity, but also a bit of nervousness about the responsibility." Or they might say, "It sounded like there was frustration in that situation, but also determination to solve the problem."

This exercise often surprises both participants.

The speaker realizes that their emotional experience has been recognized without needing to repeat or defend it. The listener discovers how much emotional information is present in ordinary conversations.

When people feel that their emotions are acknowledged accurately, something shifts in the relationship. They become more open and trusting. The conversation becomes less about proving a point and more about understanding each other.

Practicing Level-3 listening regularly can change how others respond to you within a short period of time.

Friends may begin sharing thoughts more openly because they feel heard. Colleagues may approach you for discussion because conversations with you feel constructive rather than rushed. Even conflicts may become easier to resolve because emotional signals are recognized earlier.

Listening in this way does not require extraordinary talent. It requires presence.

When you give someone your full attention and listen for both words and emotions, the quality of the interaction changes. People notice the difference immediately.

In many cases, that difference becomes one of the strongest foundations for trust and influence.

7.3 — Influence Without Manipulation

Influence is often misunderstood.

Some people associate the word with persuasion techniques designed to push others toward a desired outcome. In this interpretation, influence can appear manipulative or self-serving. It may involve strategic language, psychological pressure, or carefully timed arguments.

Yet influence in its healthiest form looks very different.

Ethical influence does not rely on deception or coercion. Instead, it emerges from clarity, trust, and shared understanding. When people trust your intentions and understand your reasoning, they are far more willing to consider your ideas.

The difference between influence and manipulation lies primarily in transparency.

Manipulation involves hidden agendas. The person attempting to persuade others conceals their true intentions or presents information selectively to control the outcome. The other party may feel pressured or misled once the situation becomes clear.

Influence, by contrast, involves mutual benefit and open communication. The person advocating for an idea expresses their reasoning clearly while respecting the other person's autonomy. Instead of forcing agreement, they invite collaboration.

This distinction matters because relationships rarely survive manipulation intact. Even if the immediate objective is achieved, trust erodes when people feel they have been pushed rather than respected.

Influence built on emotional intelligence follows three simple principles.

The first principle is emotional validation.

Before people consider your perspective, they need to feel that their own concerns have been acknowledged. If someone feels ignored or dismissed, they are unlikely to engage with your ideas openly.

Emotional validation does not mean agreeing with everything the other person says. It means recognizing the emotion behind their position.

For example, imagine discussing a new proposal with a colleague who appears skeptical. Instead of responding immediately with arguments, you might begin by acknowledging their concern.

You could say, “It sounds like you’re worried about the workload this change might create.” That statement does not concede the debate. It simply signals that their perspective has been heard.

Once people feel understood, they become more receptive to dialogue.

The second principle involves creating a shared frame.

Arguments often fail because each person approaches the conversation from a different perspective. One person focuses on efficiency, another on stability, and a third on long-term strategy. When these perspectives clash, discussions become fragmented.

Creating a shared frame means identifying a common objective that both parties value.

For example, instead of presenting your idea as a personal preference, you might frame it in terms of a goal the group already supports. “We both want the project to succeed within the deadline. This approach could help us reduce delays.”

By aligning the discussion with a shared objective, the conversation moves away from personal positions and toward collective outcomes.

The third principle involves commitment through choice rather than pressure.

People resist ideas when they feel forced into agreement. Psychological pressure often produces short-term compliance but long-term resentment.

Instead of pushing for immediate commitment, effective influence invites participation.

You might say, "What parts of this idea seem useful to you?" or "How would you adjust this approach so it fits your priorities?"

These questions transform persuasion into collaboration. The other person becomes part of the solution rather than a target of persuasion.

When people contribute to shaping an idea, they develop a sense of ownership. The decision feels shared rather than imposed.

Influence grounded in these principles creates stronger relationships over time. Instead of convincing people through pressure, you engage them through understanding and transparency.

Colleagues become more willing to support your proposals because they trust your intentions. Friends and partners feel respected rather than controlled.

Over time, your influence grows naturally because people associate your communication with fairness and clarity.

This approach also aligns with the emotional intelligence skills developed throughout the book.

Awareness helps you notice emotional signals in conversations. The pause prevents impulsive reactions during disagreement. Empathy allows you to understand the other person's perspective. Trust grows through consistent respect and reliability.

Influence then becomes a natural extension of these skills.

You advocate for your ideas confidently, but you also remain open to the perspectives of others. Conversations remain honest without becoming confrontational.

The result is communication that produces progress without sacrificing integrity.

And in the long run, that form of influence proves far more powerful than manipulation ever could.

Chapter 8 — Design Your Environment for Success

8.1 — You Are Your Context

When people talk about change, they often focus on personal strength. The conversation usually revolves around discipline, determination, or motivation. If someone struggles to maintain a habit, the explanation often sounds similar: they simply need more willpower.

This belief is deeply ingrained in modern culture. Stories about success frequently emphasize individuals who pushed through obstacles using sheer determination. While effort certainly matters, the emphasis on willpower alone overlooks something far more powerful.

Human behavior is strongly shaped by context.

The environments you inhabit—your physical surroundings, your daily routines, and the people around you—constantly influence your decisions. These influences operate quietly in the background, often without conscious awareness. Because they are subtle, people underestimate their power.

Yet research across psychology, behavioral economics, and neuroscience repeatedly shows the same pattern. Behavior changes more reliably when the environment changes.

To understand this idea, imagine two different scenarios.

In the first scenario, someone decides to eat healthier. They rely on willpower alone. Their kitchen remains filled with convenient snacks, sugary drinks, and highly processed foods. When hunger appears late in the evening, these options are the easiest to reach.

Each decision becomes a battle between intention and temptation.

In the second scenario, the same person adjusts their environment. Fresh fruit sits in a visible bowl on the counter. Pre-prepared healthy meals occupy the front of the refrigerator. Snacks that once triggered impulsive eating are no longer present.

Now the decision requires far less effort.

The goal has not changed, but the context has.

In the first scenario, the environment constantly challenges the intention. In the second, the environment quietly supports it. The difference lies not in personal strength but in the structure of the surroundings.

This principle extends far beyond nutrition.

Consider productivity. A person who attempts to focus while their phone displays constant notifications must resist distractions repeatedly. Another person who silences notifications and places the phone out of reach encounters far fewer interruptions.

The work itself may require the same mental effort, but the environment determines how often focus is disrupted.

The same pattern appears in exercise habits, financial decisions, communication styles, and even emotional reactions.

Humans tend to follow the path that requires the least friction.

When the desired behavior is easy and visible, it becomes more likely. When the undesired behavior is convenient, it becomes difficult to avoid. The brain naturally conserves energy by choosing the simplest option available in the moment.

This is why environment design often matters more than willpower.

Willpower functions like a limited resource. When you rely on it repeatedly throughout the day, it becomes depleted. Each decision requires mental effort, and after enough decisions the mind begins seeking easier alternatives.

Environment design changes the equation entirely.

Instead of relying on constant self-control, you shape your surroundings so the best choice becomes the default choice.

This concept is sometimes described as default architecture.

Default architecture refers to the way options are arranged within a system. The default option is the one that occurs automatically if no additional effort is applied.

For example, when a computer installs software with default settings, most users accept those settings because changing them requires extra steps. The default becomes the path of least resistance.

Human behavior operates in a similar way.

If the default option in your environment encourages distraction, unhealthy habits, or procrastination, those behaviors will appear frequently. If the default encourages focus, movement, or thoughtful decision-making, those behaviors become easier to maintain.

Designing your environment therefore means intentionally shaping the default path.

Imagine someone who wants to read more regularly. If books remain hidden on a distant shelf while the television remote sits on the coffee table, the environment quietly encourages screen time.

But if a book rests on the table where the remote once sat, the default behavior shifts slightly. The book becomes the easiest form of entertainment within reach.

These small adjustments may seem trivial, but their effects accumulate over time.

The same principle applies to routines. If the first activity of the morning involves checking messages, the day begins with reactive attention. The mind responds to external demands before establishing personal priorities.

If the morning routine begins with a brief planning moment instead, the day starts with intention rather than reaction.

Default architecture also includes the people you interact with regularly.

Social environments influence behavior more strongly than many individuals realize. People tend to adopt the norms of the groups around them. When friends value health, learning, or constructive conversation, those behaviors feel natural. When the social environment encourages constant distraction or negativity, maintaining positive habits becomes more difficult.

This does not mean abandoning relationships, but it does mean recognizing the influence they carry.

For example, someone who joins a group where regular exercise is common may find that the habit develops almost automatically. The activity becomes part of shared culture rather than a solitary effort.

Similarly, a workplace where colleagues openly discuss ideas and support each other's progress creates an atmosphere that encourages learning.

Your context quietly shapes your expectations of what is normal.

Once you recognize this influence, you begin to see your environment differently.

The spaces you inhabit, the routines you repeat, and the conversations you engage in are not neutral. They are systems that either support your goals or undermine them.

Consider a typical workday.

If your desk is cluttered with unfinished tasks and notifications appear constantly, the environment signals urgency and fragmentation. Focus becomes difficult because attention is pulled in multiple directions.

If the workspace contains only the materials necessary for the current task, the environment signals clarity. The absence of competing stimuli allows concentration to deepen.

Even lighting, noise, and physical comfort influence behavior. A bright, organized workspace often encourages alertness and productivity, while a chaotic or uncomfortable space encourages distraction.

The key insight is that behavior rarely exists in isolation.

Every action occurs within a context. When that context aligns with your goals, progress becomes smoother. When the context conflicts with your goals, effort increases dramatically.

Understanding this principle leads to an important question.

Is your current environment helping you move toward the life you want, or is it quietly steering you in another direction?

Many people never ask this question. They attempt to change habits while leaving their surroundings unchanged. As a result, they struggle against invisible friction.

But when you begin auditing your environment, patterns appear quickly.

You may notice that certain locations encourage focus while others trigger distraction. Certain routines support progress while others delay it. Certain social interactions energize you while others drain your motivation.

These observations reveal whether your environment acts as an ally or a saboteur.

An ally environment reduces friction around positive behaviors. It makes healthy actions visible and accessible. It removes unnecessary obstacles that require constant willpower to overcome.

A saboteur environment does the opposite. It fills daily life with cues that trigger unhelpful habits. It hides beneficial actions behind layers of inconvenience.

The good news is that environments are adjustable.

You do not need dramatic changes to begin shifting the balance. Small adjustments often produce noticeable improvements. Moving a book into sight, silencing notifications, preparing tools for the next day's work, or adjusting the layout of a workspace can alter the default path.

Over time these adjustments accumulate.

Instead of fighting your surroundings, you begin collaborating with them. Your environment becomes a quiet partner in the process of change.

As the chapters ahead explore further, designing supportive contexts will become a central strategy for sustaining the habits and emotional intelligence skills you have developed so far.

Because when the environment works with you rather than against you, progress requires far less struggle.

And that realization changes the way you approach every goal moving forward.

8.2 — The Five Circles Audit

Once you understand that behavior is strongly influenced by context, the next question becomes practical: how do you redesign that context in a meaningful way?

Many people attempt to change their environment randomly. They reorganize a desk, download a productivity application, or join a new group without thinking about how these elements interact. Some changes help, others fade quickly, and the overall impact remains unclear.

A more effective approach is to examine the environment systematically.

One useful framework is what we can call the Five Circles Audit. The idea is simple. Your daily life operates inside several overlapping environments, each shaping your behavior in different ways. By examining these circles deliberately, you can identify where friction exists and where small adjustments might create significant change.

The five circles include your physical space, digital environment, social circle, daily routines, and information diet. Each one quietly influences decisions throughout the day.

The first circle is your physical space.

Your surroundings constantly send signals about how you should behave. A cluttered desk suggests unfinished work. A comfortable reading chair invites reflection. A kitchen counter filled with snacks encourages impulsive eating. None of these signals are dramatic, yet they accumulate over time.

Begin by walking through the spaces where you spend the most time. Notice what each environment encourages by default.

If you want to work more effectively, look at the layout of your workspace. Does the environment make focus easier or harder? Are the tools you need immediately available, or hidden behind layers of inconvenience?

Small adjustments can create noticeable improvements. One of the simplest upgrades involves removing friction around the behavior you want to repeat. If reading is a goal, place a book where you usually reach for your phone. If exercise matters, keep equipment visible rather than stored away.

Another adjustment involves reducing distractions. Clearing visual clutter from a workspace often improves concentration because the mind receives fewer competing signals.

Finally, consider adding cues that reinforce desired habits. A notebook placed beside your desk may remind you to reflect at the end of the day. A water bottle on the table may encourage healthier routines.

These changes require little effort yet produce immediate environmental signals.

The second circle is your digital environment.

Modern life involves constant interaction with digital tools, and those tools are designed to capture attention. Notifications, messages, and algorithm-driven content compete for your focus throughout the day.

Without intentional boundaries, the digital environment can become one of the strongest sources of distraction.

Begin by observing how often your attention shifts because of notifications. If messages appear continuously, concentration becomes fragmented.

One effective upgrade involves reducing the number of notifications allowed to interrupt your day. Many applications do not require immediate attention. Silencing nonessential alerts can dramatically improve focus.

Another adjustment involves organizing digital spaces around your priorities. If you open a browser and immediately see distracting content, the environment encourages procrastination. Replacing those cues with useful tools—such as a planning page or project dashboard—redirects attention toward productive actions.

A third improvement involves scheduling digital breaks rather than responding to every notification immediately. When the mind expects regular check-in periods, it becomes easier to ignore interruptions between them.

The third circle involves your social environment.

People naturally adapt to the behaviors and attitudes of the groups around them. Conversations, expectations, and shared norms shape how individuals interpret what is normal.

This does not mean every relationship must align perfectly with your goals. Diversity of perspective is valuable. However, it is useful to recognize which interactions energize progress and which ones subtly discourage it.

Consider the conversations you have most frequently. Do they revolve around ideas, growth, and solutions, or do they drift toward complaints and frustration?

One meaningful upgrade is to spend more time with individuals who encourage constructive thinking. Even occasional discussions with people who value learning or creativity can influence how you approach challenges.

Another step involves introducing topics that promote growth within existing relationships. Asking thoughtful questions about goals, projects, or interests often shifts the tone of conversation.

A third adjustment involves reducing exposure to consistently negative environments. This does not require confrontation. Sometimes it simply means spending less time in conversations that repeatedly drain energy.

The fourth circle includes daily routines.

Routines form the structure of everyday life. They determine when actions occur and how smoothly transitions happen between tasks.

When routines are unstructured, decisions appear constantly throughout the day. Each decision requires mental energy, which gradually depletes attention.

Designing routines reduces this decision fatigue.

Start by examining the beginning and end of your day. Morning and evening routines often influence everything that follows. A calm morning routine may create focus for the entire day, while a rushed beginning may produce stress that lingers.

Small upgrades can improve these transitions. Preparing materials for the next day in advance removes morning friction. Ending the evening with a brief review of priorities may clarify the next day's direction.

Another routine adjustment involves grouping similar tasks together. When activities share context, the mind moves between them more efficiently.

Finally, consider introducing short pauses between major tasks. Even a brief moment of reflection helps the mind reset before shifting focus.

The fifth circle involves your information diet.

Information shapes perception, which in turn influences decisions. The books you read, the media you consume, and the conversations you follow all contribute to how you interpret the world.

If most incoming information emphasizes conflict or negativity, it becomes difficult to maintain clarity and optimism. If information sources encourage learning and perspective, the mind becomes more adaptable.

Auditing your information diet means asking where your attention goes each day.

Are you consuming material that expands understanding, or primarily reacting to headlines and distractions?

One upgrade may involve replacing a portion of passive media consumption with intentional learning. Reading thoughtful articles, books, or listening to educational content can shift mental energy toward curiosity.

Another improvement involves limiting exposure to sources that consistently provoke emotional reactions without providing insight.

A final step might involve scheduling time for reflection after absorbing new ideas. Reflection turns information into understanding.

After completing the Five Circles Audit, patterns often become clear.

You may notice that a few small changes could significantly improve your environment. Perhaps a reorganized workspace, adjusted notification settings, a new conversation habit, and a structured morning routine would reduce daily friction dramatically.

The goal is not to redesign every aspect of life at once. Instead, identify five to ten changes that offer the greatest impact with reasonable effort.

These adjustments become the first steps in transforming your environment into an ally rather than a hidden obstacle.

Chapter 9 — Day 41 and Beyond

9.1 — What You Have Built

When you first opened this book, the journey ahead may have felt abstract. Forty days can seem like a short period of time, and personal growth is often described as something that unfolds slowly across years. Yet meaningful change rarely begins with dramatic transformations. It begins with consistent attention to small shifts in awareness, thinking, and behavior.

Over the past forty days, you have practiced exactly that.

Instead of trying to change everything at once, you focused on a sequence of capabilities that gradually reinforced one another. Each chapter added a layer of understanding and skill. Individually these steps may have seemed modest, but together they form a system that influences how you interpret challenges, interact with others, and pursue your goals.

Looking back across the journey, the progression followed four distinct phases.

The first phase focused on awareness.

Before meaningful change can occur, people must learn to observe their internal world clearly. Many emotional reactions happen so quickly that they appear automatic. Frustration emerges before the mind has time to examine it. Anxiety appears without explanation. Conversations become tense before anyone realizes why.

The early chapters helped you slow down this process.

You practiced identifying emotions with greater precision instead of relying on vague labels such as stress or irritation. You learned to notice the physical signals your body produces when emotions begin forming—changes in breathing, tension in the jaw or shoulders, subtle shifts in posture.

You also explored the narratives that accompany these emotions. The mind constantly tells stories about what events mean. Some of those stories protect you, but others quietly limit what you believe is possible.

By recognizing these patterns, you developed the ability to pause and examine them rather than accepting them automatically.

Awareness may appear simple, but it represents a powerful shift. When you see emotional reactions forming in real time, you gain the opportunity to guide them.

The second phase built on that awareness by introducing regulation.

Recognizing emotions is only the beginning. The next challenge involves responding to them deliberately rather than impulsively.

You practiced creating a pause between trigger and reaction. The six-second rule allowed the initial surge of emotion to pass before decisions were made. Breathing techniques, physical anchors, and deliberate counting provided tools for stabilizing the nervous system during stressful moments.

Through repeated practice, you began experiencing the difference between reacting and responding.

Instead of allowing frustration or anxiety to determine your words immediately, you created space for intention. Conversations that once escalated quickly could now unfold with greater calm. Difficult moments became opportunities for thoughtful action rather than impulsive defense.

This capacity for regulation is one of the foundations of emotional intelligence. It protects relationships, improves decision-making, and strengthens confidence during uncertainty.

The third phase introduced reframing.

Once you learned to pause and observe your emotional reactions, it became possible to examine the stories behind them more carefully. Many of the thoughts that appear during stressful moments are interpretations rather than facts.

You practiced challenging these interpretations through structured reflection. The three-column method encouraged you to distinguish between situations, automatic thoughts, and evidence-based alternatives. Over time, this process weakened limiting narratives and replaced them with more balanced perspectives.

Reframing also transformed how you interpret setbacks.

Instead of allowing failure to define identity, you learned to treat experiences as sources of information. The after-action review process helped convert mistakes into structured learning events. Resilience became less about avoiding difficulty and more about responding constructively when difficulty appeared.

This shift changed the relationship between effort and outcome. Challenges stopped feeling like verdicts about your ability and began functioning as feedback within a larger process of improvement.

The fourth phase focused on integration.

Emotional intelligence does not exist only within personal reflection. It influences how you communicate, collaborate, and build trust with others.

You explored the importance of reading social dynamics in conversations and meetings. Social awareness allowed you to notice signals that often remain unspoken—changes in tone, shifts in attention, and subtle reactions that reveal what people are feeling.

You also practiced listening at a deeper level. Instead of hearing only the content of someone's message, you learned to recognize the emotions behind it. This skill strengthens relationships because people feel understood when their experiences are acknowledged accurately.

Communication frameworks such as the STATE method provided structure for difficult conversations. Instead of avoiding tension or allowing emotions to escalate, you developed language patterns that encourage honesty and dialogue at the same time.

You also examined how trust develops through consistent actions. Small deposits of reliability, transparency, and acknowledgment accumulate into strong relationships over time.

Beyond interpersonal skills, integration extended to the design of your environment. You learned that behavior does not occur in isolation. Physical spaces, digital habits, social influences, and daily routines all shape the decisions you make.

By adjusting these environments intentionally, you reduced the amount of willpower required to maintain progress. Goals became more sustainable because the context supporting them improved.

Finally, you explored the power of accountability. When commitments become visible to others, motivation strengthens. Shared expectations create a structure that helps maintain consistency during difficult moments.

Each of these capabilities now forms part of your toolkit.

You can identify emotions with greater precision.
You can pause before reacting under pressure.
You can challenge limiting narratives and replace them with more balanced interpretations.
You can navigate difficult conversations with clarity and respect.
You can design environments that support your goals.
You can build trust and accountability structures that sustain progress.

These skills do not represent isolated techniques. They work together.

Awareness supports regulation. Regulation allows reframing. Reframing strengthens communication. Communication builds trust. Trust reinforces supportive environments. Supportive environments make growth easier to maintain.

The system becomes self-reinforcing.

At this point in the journey, it is valuable to pause and measure how far you have come.

At the beginning of the book, you were invited to reflect on several questions related to emotional awareness, emotional regulation, and mindset. Those questions served as a baseline for your starting point.

Now is the time to revisit them.

Consider again how quickly you recognize emotional reactions when they appear. Do you notice them earlier than before?

Reflect on how you respond when pressure rises. Are you more capable of pausing and choosing your response deliberately?

Think about how you interpret setbacks or criticism. Do you approach them with greater curiosity and flexibility?

You may choose to rate these areas again using the same scale you used earlier. Even small changes in these scores represent meaningful progress because they indicate shifts in daily habits.

Growth in emotional intelligence rarely appears as dramatic breakthroughs. Instead, it reveals itself through subtle changes in how situations feel.

Conversations that once triggered immediate defensiveness may now feel manageable. Challenges that once produced discouragement may now stimulate problem-solving. Goals that once seemed overwhelming may now appear achievable through structured effort.

These differences accumulate.

They influence how you approach work, relationships, and personal ambitions. Over time, the small habits practiced during these forty days become part of how you naturally operate.

The most important insight to remember is that this process does not end on day forty.

The skills you have developed are not temporary exercises. They are practices that continue strengthening with repetition. The more often you pause before reacting, the more natural that pause becomes. The more frequently you examine your narratives, the easier it becomes to replace limiting interpretations with constructive ones.

Growth in emotional intelligence resembles physical fitness in one important way.

You do not complete it once.

You maintain it through ongoing practice.

Day forty-one therefore represents not an ending but a transition. You now possess a framework for understanding your emotions, guiding your thoughts, and shaping your environment in ways that support meaningful progress.

What you build next will depend on how you continue applying these capabilities.

And the most encouraging part of the journey is that the tools you need are already in your hands.

9.2 — The Maintenance Mindset

Reaching the end of a structured program can produce a powerful feeling of completion. After weeks of reflection, practice, and adjustment, it is natural to pause and think, *I've done it. I've changed.*

That sense of progress is important. You have invested time and attention into developing skills that many people never deliberately practice. You have learned how to recognize emotions earlier, regulate reactions more effectively, question limiting narratives, communicate with greater clarity, and design environments that support better decisions.

But there is a subtle psychological trap waiting at this moment.

It appears whenever growth is mistaken for a destination.

Many personal development efforts lose momentum not because the material was ineffective but because people believe the transformation should now sustain itself automatically. Once the structured effort ends, attention gradually shifts back to the usual demands of daily life. The practices that created progress become less frequent. Reflection disappears first, then intentional habits slowly fade.

Within a few months, many of the insights that once felt powerful become distant memories.

This pattern is not a failure of discipline. It is a misunderstanding of how change works.

Emotional intelligence and mindset development operate much like physical fitness. A person can build strength through focused training, but the strength remains only if the body continues to move. Without maintenance, even well-developed abilities gradually weaken.

The same principle applies to emotional skills.

Awareness fades if you stop noticing internal signals. Regulation becomes inconsistent if the pause is no longer practiced. Narrative reframing becomes rare if automatic thoughts go unquestioned again.

The solution is not to repeat the entire forty-day program indefinitely. Instead, the goal is to adopt what might be called a maintenance mindset.

A maintenance mindset recognizes that growth is a continuous practice rather than a finished achievement. The purpose is not constant effort but periodic attention.

Just as physical health can be maintained with a few regular workouts each week, emotional intelligence can remain strong through small, consistent check-ins.

One practical way to sustain progress is through a weekly fifteen-minute review.

Fifteen minutes may sound almost too small to matter, but the power of the routine lies in its consistency. When reflection becomes a regular habit, it prevents the gradual drift back toward unconscious patterns.

The review includes three brief components: an emotional intelligence check-in, a mindset review, and an environment scan.

The first part of the routine is the EQ check-in.

During this moment, reflect on the emotional patterns you experienced during the past week. Ask yourself a few simple questions.

Were there moments when strong emotions appeared quickly? Did you notice them early, or did you realize their influence only afterward? Were there situations where the pause between trigger and reaction helped you respond more thoughtfully?

You are not searching for perfection. The purpose of the check-in is simply to maintain awareness.

Sometimes you will notice progress. Perhaps you handled a difficult conversation calmly or recognized frustration before it escalated. Other weeks may reveal areas where reactions still happen quickly.

Both observations are useful because they keep the learning process active.

The second component is the mindset review.

During this step, examine the stories that influenced your thinking during the week. Did you encounter a challenge that triggered familiar doubts or assumptions?

For example, perhaps a project became difficult and your mind briefly suggested that the effort might not succeed. Instead of accepting that thought automatically, you can ask whether it represents a fact or an interpretation.

Revisit the reframing skills you practiced earlier in the journey. Look at the situation again and ask what evidence supports the interpretation and what alternative explanations might exist.

This short review prevents limiting narratives from becoming permanent again. By questioning them regularly, you maintain cognitive flexibility.

The third component of the routine is the environment scan.

Your surroundings evolve constantly. New habits appear, digital tools change, schedules shift, and relationships develop. An environment that supported your goals last month may gradually become cluttered or distracting again.

Take a few minutes to observe whether your context still aligns with your intentions.

Is your workspace still arranged in a way that encourages focus? Are digital notifications creeping back into your day more frequently? Are routines drifting away from the structure that once helped you begin mornings or close evenings with intention?

If something feels misaligned, identify a small adjustment you can make during the coming week.

The adjustment does not need to be dramatic. Sometimes moving a notebook, silencing an application, or adjusting a routine slightly restores the supportive structure.

Together these three steps—emotional awareness, narrative reflection, and environmental alignment—form a simple maintenance system.

In fifteen minutes each week, you reconnect with the practices that created progress during the forty-day journey.

The effect of this routine is subtle but powerful.

Instead of allowing months to pass before noticing that habits have faded, you detect small shifts early. Corrections remain easy because the system never drifts too far from its foundation.

This approach also changes how you interpret setbacks in the future.

Instead of viewing them as evidence that progress has disappeared, you treat them as signals that a brief reset is needed. The maintenance routine becomes a compass that keeps you oriented even when life becomes busy.

The goal is not constant self-analysis. It is periodic awareness.

When the maintenance mindset becomes part of your life, growth remains active without requiring intense effort.

The investment you made during these forty days continues producing value because the system supporting it remains alive.

9.3 — Your Next Move

As you reach the end of this journey, one final step can make everything you have learned far more durable.

It involves sharing the knowledge.

Within the next forty-eight hours, choose one person in your life and teach them a skill from this book.

The skill does not need to be complex. It could be the six-second pause that prevents emotional reactions from escalating. It might be the three-column reframing method that helps challenge automatic thoughts. It could be the listening technique that focuses on emotions rather than just words.

What matters is not which skill you choose but the act of explaining it.

When people teach something they have learned, their own understanding deepens dramatically. This phenomenon is often called the "teach to lock" principle.

The human brain organizes knowledge differently when preparing to teach it. Instead of remembering information passively, you begin arranging it in a way that another person can understand. You search for clear examples, simple explanations, and practical steps.

This process strengthens memory and comprehension at the same time.

Imagine explaining the six-second pause to a friend or colleague. You might describe how emotional reactions occur quickly because of the brain's threat detection system. You might explain that pausing for a few seconds allows the rational mind to regain influence.

As you describe the idea, you reinforce your own awareness of the technique.

Later, when you encounter a stressful moment, the explanation you shared becomes easier to recall because you have already organized it in your mind.

Teaching also creates a subtle form of accountability.

When you show someone a skill and encourage them to try it, you become more aware of your own behavior. If you recommended pausing before reacting, you will likely notice whether you are practicing the same habit.

The act of sharing therefore strengthens both memory and commitment.

Another important benefit appears in the relationship itself.

When you introduce someone to a useful skill, the conversation often becomes deeper. Instead of discussing only surface-level topics, you explore ideas about emotions, mindset, and growth. These conversations can strengthen trust and mutual support.

Over time, the person you teach may begin sharing their own experiences applying the skill. The two of you create a small environment of shared learning.

That environment reinforces the habits you developed during the past forty days.

The person you choose does not need to be someone seeking dramatic change. It could be a friend curious about stress management, a colleague interested in communication, or a family member navigating a difficult situation.

Simply explain one concept clearly and invite them to try it.

You might say something like, "I've been practicing a small technique for managing emotional reactions. When something stressful happens, I pause for a few seconds before responding. It helps me think more clearly."

The explanation may take only a few minutes, but the impact can last much longer.

Because every time you teach a concept, you strengthen it within yourself.

This final step represents an important shift.

Throughout the book, you have focused primarily on developing your own awareness and habits. Now you move from learning to sharing. Growth becomes something that spreads beyond individual practice.

In many ways, this is how meaningful change continues.

Skills become stronger when they exist inside communities rather than isolated individuals. When multiple people practice awareness, thoughtful communication, and supportive environments, the culture around them begins to shift.

Conversations become calmer. Decisions become clearer. Relationships become more constructive.

Your influence in that process may begin with something as simple as explaining a small technique to one person.

From there, the impact expands.

As you move beyond day forty, remember one final truth.

The distance between the person you were when you began this journey and the person you are becoming now is not determined by talent or intelligence.

It is determined by emotional skill and mental framing.

You have practiced recognizing emotions rather than being controlled by them. You have learned to question limiting stories rather than accepting them automatically. You have developed the ability to pause, reflect, communicate, and design environments that support progress.

These abilities are not temporary insights.

They are tools.

And from this point forward, they belong to you.

www.ingramcontent.com/pod-product-compliance
Ingram Content Group UK Ltd.
Pitfield, Milton Keynes, MK11 3LW, UK
UKHW012248290726
14090UKWH00013B/541

9 798903 298822